We Came,
We Saw, We Converted

The Lighter Side
of Orthodoxy in America

Fr. Joseph Huneycutt

CONCILIAR
PRESS

Ben Lomond, California

WE CAME, WE SAW, WE CONVERTED:
The Lighter Side of Orthodoxy in America
© Copyright 2009 by Joseph Huneycutt

Published by
    Conciliar Press
    (A division of Conciliar Media Ministries)
    P.O. Box 76
    Ben Lomond, California 95005-0076

Printed in the United States of America

ISBN 10: 0-9822770-8-3
ISBN 13: 978-0-9822770-8-9

In memory of Archimandrite Damian (Hart)
1931–2009

*"We're not Orthodox in order to
escape the gaping jaws of hell.
We're Orthodox in thanksgiving for
what God has done for us in the Incarnation."*

Eternal Memory!

Contents

Part IV:
JUST GIMME THAT OL' COUNTRY RELIGION ... *page 129*

Bless Your Heart—*Smallah, Smallah, Smallah!*

He's in a Better Place . . . than Dixie?

Letters from the Old Country

When the Roll Is Called up Yonder

An Empty Church Is a Peaceful Church

A Funny Thing Happened on the Way to Phronema

Part V:
SAINTS, SINGERS, AND SUPERHEROES .... *page 171*

Constantine: He Built the City, but He Didn't Write the Song!

People for the Ethical Treatment of . . . Dragons?

Saint Elvis?

Acknowledgements

We Came, We Saw, We Converted is a collection of stories taken from episodes of the *Orthodixie* podcast on Ancient Faith Radio. This collection's goal is to present a humorous look at the pluses, minuses, joys, pitfalls, and struggles of perpetual conversion within an Orthodox Christian worldview.

I am indebted to the vision, patience, forbearance, and encouragement of John and Tonya Maddex and the whole crew at Ancient Faith Radio, especially my podcast producer, Ron Smith. Also, my "t"s would be less crossed, my "i"s less dotted were it not for the helpful eyes of Susan Engelhardt.

I must also thank my wife, Elizabeth, and my children, Mary Catherine, Basil, and Helen. They have tolerated many nights of my hogging loveseat and laptop in order to write podcast scripts. They have also put up with weekly evacuations, allowing me to record—*and* served as faithful guinea pigs, listening to each episode of the *Orthodixie* podcast before uploading to Ancient Faith Radio.

Students of the art of comedy know that for humor to work, it must bear some semblance to the truth. One truth about humor: it's usually at someone's expense. Something you find funny, someone else finds offensive, and vice versa. With that in mind, in advance, I beg your forgiveness.

Part I

Orthodoxy in America

Shut Up, Go Home, Pray More

Back in 1995, while attending a wonderful gathering of Roman Catholics, Evangelicals, and Eastern Orthodox in a conference called "Not of This World," in Aiken, South Carolina, Bishop Kallistos (Ware) was entertaining questions following his presentation. There was a line of folks patiently waiting for their turn to approach the floor microphone, where some poor fellow had worn out his welcome—standing there for way too long, obviously enjoying the sound of his own voice. You know the type: two pocket protectors, ten ink pens, tape on his eyeglasses, and three wristwatches. I do believe his diatribe before the bishop and the assembly included everything from the pyramids to dinosaurs, Sasquatch, and intergalactic travel.

It was about this time that a delightful old priest in front of me turned around and said, "Back in seminary, I had a professor who would tell a guy like this, 'Shut up, go home, pray more.'"

My friend and I could hardly contain our laughter. Now that's a viable slogan! *Shut up, go home, pray more.* Forgive me, but we're all susceptible to the temptation of being full of ourselves, puffed up, impressed by our own words.

Years before, while in seminary, I was traveling to the airport with a young man, a non-Christian, who was trying to educate me on how the world was actually being run by three people, members of some elite group, who regularly counseled with space aliens (who made frequent stops on planet Earth), etc.

Somewhere in the midst of all this, on a whim and with no back story at all, I said, "I think you need to lay off the dope."

"What?" he asked.

"The dope," I said. "Stop smoking pot."

He then said, "You know, you're right. I should."

He filled me in on his story and his struggle to quit. He then said, "How did you know?"

I said, "I didn't. I've just never known anyone who believed all that stuff who wasn't hooked on something."

Do you know—just a footnote here—the guy eventually quit the dope, got his life straight, and got married? Amazing. It's funny how a single event, even a brief encounter, can change one's life.

Sometimes these events are presented as negative, only to be turned round to bear good fruit. Other times, the event may be one of awesome wonder that leaves us speechless, lacking words but not tears: the birth of a child, the sight of your bride, news of a promotion . . . God. Sometimes God enters the picture and changes everything.

There's St. Paul, knocked from his horse by a vision on the road, never to return to the Saul he was.

There's the monk who walks away from a life of sinful debauchery and spends his days reading words of praise and repentance high on a hill in a monastery.

There's a maiden in Nazareth whose daily routine is interrupted by a being named Gabriel bearing astounding news—but she kept it, pondering his words in her heart.

There's the mother weeping before her icons, praying for her wayward daughter, the one who miraculously ends up okay. (This mother, too, ponders God's wonders in her heart.)

There's the soldier whose job it is to pick up the torn-apart bodies on the battlefield—only to return home, drink Mr. Pibb, play catch, eat soda crackers, and never talk about that war again.

There's the car pulling off the road in Northern Wisconsin, the driver captivated by the otherworldly beauty of the Northern Lights. He wonders how great the Lord's return will be.

There's the saintly abbot who dies on his bed, only to come back to life shortly afterward, claiming he's been shown the glories of heaven. He stays the rest of his days in his cell repenting in order once again to return to that place.

There's the one, the two, the three, the five hundred who saw the Lord after He had been raised from the dead.

All of these can relate: *Shut up, go home, pray more.*

Sometimes, silence. Silence, much like an empty tomb, is fuller than any words could ever be. Essentially, it all boils down to what the late Jaroslav Pelikan said: "If Christ is risen, nothing else matters. And if Christ is not risen—nothing else matters." Where you fall within that quotation makes all the difference.

Besides, sometimes what we hear is not what was actually said. Many times, I'm reminded of something that someone heard me say in a sermon which, to my knowledge, I have never said in my life. It's nice when what they heard me say is worth repeating!

A while back someone heard me on Ancient Faith Radio and emailed me saying, "You didn't sound nearly as Southern as I expected." Someone else soon commented saying just the opposite.

But, in truth, we all have accents. Some of us may sound more like television than others, but we all have accents. It's sometimes the case that what we say is misheard, in part, due to accent—our inflection, or lack thereof, of the spoken word.

For example, when I was making arrangements to move from North Carolina to Houston, I was speaking with a parishioner of St. George who was from the Middle East. In trying to get the email info copied down correctly, I made him repeat the address. To my ears, he said, "L as in Nancy . . . H as in Fred . . ." Oh, my! I made the sign of the cross and thought, "O Lord, this is going to be a challenge!"

Months later, while giving Communion, I had a similar problem. Of course we like to commune the faithful using their Christian names, and in a large parish, it helps if folks assist the process by saying their name at the chalice. On this particular day, a man brought forth his young son. I asked, "What's his name?"

The man picked the boy up and said something rather loudly. I didn't quite understand the accent and said, "I'm sorry, what?"

He probably didn't understand the question and repeated what he'd already said, even louder. In my confusion and haste, I quickly repeated what I'd heard him say only to find myself, forgive me, fighting off the giggles.

When I walked back into the altar, someone asked, "What are you smiling about?"

I said, "I just communed OpenYaMouth!"

There have been many opportunities like that with me, a Southerner, serving in a parish made up predominantly of Middle Easterners. I can often repeat exactly what my ears heard only to be corrected, again and again.

We love each other. So it's all good. But it does give one pause. It's humbling to think of how little we really know about anything, thanks to our struggle to understand each other. Even when we share an accent, words can get us in trouble. People will even say we said things we never said!

Once, while starting a mission in North Carolina, I was interviewed for the local paper. As often happens, most of what I said ended up not being printed in the article, while some things I didn't say made it in instead. For instance, the article ended by saying that, when asked what resources one needed to start an Orthodox mission, Fr. Joseph said, "There's no book like the Good Book."

Y'all? I promise. I never said that. But it brings me back to my point: *Shut up, go home, pray more.* Yes, "that'll preach," as they say, and you preach most what you most need to learn.

That said, I hope you enjoy the book. The following stories are all adapted from the *Orthodixie* podcast on Ancient Faith Radio. Somewhere, amid the silliness and accents, may it find kinship with the Subject of the Good Book.

(I'll save "shut up, go home, pray more" until the end.)

Enjoy!

What It Takes

Do you have what it takes? That's the question: *Do you have what it takes?*

It was years ago, perhaps in another reality, but a man came up to me and asked, "Do you have what it takes?"

I said, "What are you talking about?"

"What it takes?" he repeated. Then he showed me a book. I looked down and saw the title of the book. Written large in Sharpie on duct tape over a floppy leather cover, it read, *What It Takes.*

I reached out for *What It Takes,* and he quickly put it behind his back. I said, "Let me see it!"

He said, "What?"

I said, "Give me *What It Takes!*"

"What do you mean?" he said.

"*What It Takes.* You showed me a book, you said it was *What It Takes,* and now you've hidden it from me!"

"Well, that's my point," he said. "You don't have it."

"I know," I said. "May I have it?"

He said, "You can only have it with me attached to it."

"What?"

"*What It Takes!*"

"What do you mean?" I asked.

"You said," he said, "that you wanted *What It Takes*—I'm willing to give it to you."

"Well, okay! Give me *What It Takes!*"

"Ah, not so fast, my friend; you must do as I say."

17

"Forget it," I said, "Maybe I don't have what it takes."

But it bugged me, you know—that I didn't have what it takes. So I kept looking. I eventually found a group of people that said *All It Took* is what I had; sort of like, *I'm Okay, You're Okay*. And that was—*okay*, for a while anyway.

Yet, after a while, it seemed that something was lacking. I began to doubt that that group really understood the *What* it was that they were supposed to, uh, *Take*; you know, *What It Takes!* So I left. I wandered hither and yon.

Some very nice people told me maybe I could find *What It Takes* on some hip religious radio stations. So I tuned in. First there was Radio Station KWIT—real contemporary: "Skiddlie-be-bop-we-rock-a Scooby-doo, you know the Bible says so—Jesus loves you!"

Nah. Not for me.

Then there was Radio Station WITF, which stood for What It Takes Fundamentally, or maybe it was What It Takes Funky. They played a song that sounded like Amy Winehouse's "Rehab": "The Devil says to go to Hades . . . I won't go, no, no . . ."

Uh, unh-uh. Sounded too much like the other stuff.

Then I met even goofier folks who couldn't even define what the word *What* meant or where *It* was. And *Take*? Well, take was all there was to this group. Take, take, take . . . gimme, gimme, gimme.

You know, like that old country song by Toby Keith, "It was all about I, it was all about Number One, O, my, me my—what I think, what I like, what I know, what I want, what I see!" It was all about *me, Me,* **Me, ME***!*

In the end, I knew that I didn't have *What It Takes,* and these people certainly didn't have it. They did say one thing, however, that piqued my curiosity. They said there was a man, up high in the mountains, a very wise man who, if I really was seeking *What It Takes*, might have an answer for me.

So I set off on a quest to quench my thirst and gain the answer to the question, "What is—do I have—*What It Takes*?"

Many days, nights, months, and years I journeyed—up, up, and up (okay, sometimes I slipped back down a mile or two), till finally I saw him: a kind of a hippie-lookin' dude, just sitting there, no joke, on top of a hill.

I felt dirty, unwashed, hungry for the Truth. I had cast off the indoctrination, for good or ill, from my youth. Now, here I was just moments away from—

"Do you have what it takes?" he asked.

And before I could answer, I noticed he had a little painting of Jesus hanging there on a wall. I said, "Jesus? You're kidding me—*Jesus*?"

"Sure," he said. "Jesus is hip."

And then I couldn't exactly hear what he was saying because, real or imagined, I was spiraling down through the ages of my life—past the New Agers who had no answers (believing themselves to be the answer); past that one group that didn't really care about *What It Takes*; past the man with the leatherbound book that he called *What It Takes* (but, of course, it was a package deal; he went with the book).

Until . . .

Thud. I landed on the flat ground, and there was the strange and mysterious man with me still. He said, "Come," and we began walking.

As we walked, he talked. He talked about Christ in a way I'd never heard before. It was getting late, and we'd walked so far we were near my house. I asked this stranger, who seemed to be going further, to dine with me at my house. And, I know this might sound strange, but there was something about the way he prayed, something about the way he took bread and blessed it, broke it, and gave it. That—that—*O. My. God.*

And then, *poof*, he was gone!

Okay, fine. That last part I stole from the Gospel story about the road to Emmaus. But isn't it funny how, over and over again, after the Resurrection, people, at first sighting, just plain don't recognize Jesus.

I remember when I was on my way to seminary, having served three years in a local Episcopal church, I decided it was time to come clean, to be perfectly honest with the priest (a man who'd been a priest for over forty years). My problem was important; I thought it might be a deal-breaker.

I said, "I love the Lord, believe in the mission of the Church, the Bible, etc., I just don't believe Jesus is God." Here was where I expected him to argue with me, to prove something to me—maybe to reject me.

He didn't bat an eye, but immediately said, "I think it's a giant leap of faith." And then he went on to talk about something else. That bugged me. The struggle itself had been bugging me for some time. But with this terse answer—*a giant leap of faith*—I was bugged even more.

A few days later, on a Sunday morning in the sacristy before service, I said, "The other day, when I told you my doubts about Jesus being God, you said it was a giant leap of faith—"

He interrupted me, saying, "Well, something happened that changed those men, His disciples who had abandoned Him at the cross. Something happened to change them into missionaries willing to, literally, give their life for the cause. Something happened. I believe they saw God."

And there it is.

And this, brothers and sisters, is *What It Takes*. Over and over again, century after century, it is recorded in the Bible and the saints' lives have borne witness:

They believed, they repented, and they were baptized.
They believed, they repented, and they were baptized.

And each and every Sunday the people of God gather to remember and celebrate the Passover (Pascha), from death to life, the Resurrection of the God-Man Christ. And, in every generation, the Lord God is made known to believers in the breaking of the bread.

We, though unworthy, stand in the presence of God and others within our temples on a regular basis and witness the greatest blessing the world will ever know: The Holy Spirit is called down upon us and upon the gifts of bread and wine; this is where transformation takes place. The elements of bread and wine are transformed by the Holy Spirit into the very Body and Blood of the God-Man Christ, and we, partakers of this mystery, are continually transformed into the very Bride of God—sons and daughters of the Father—through the Church.

Do I have *What It Takes*?

Honestly?

Nope. But He does.

It's a giant leap; I believe that's true. It's a giant leap. Christ is risen—a giant leap . . . risen from the dead—a giant leap . . . trampling down death by death—a giant leap . . . and upon those in the tombs bestowing life! Christ did, and does, *What It Takes* to save us. All we're called to do is to take that giant leap. Trust God. Be faithful. Persevere. For the God-Man, Christ, is risen from the dead and has appeared to Simon! And He is made known to His faithful disciples in the Eucharist—in the breaking of the bread.

American Orthodoxy?

One of the joys of being a podcaster on Ancient Faith Radio—in addition to the enviable salary, stock options, 401(k), and company car—is the listener correspondence. It's always nice to know someone's listening, and it proves that Orthodoxy in America, if nothing else, is making great strides in the digital world: internet radio, podcasts, blogs, and, of course, email.

Most email I receive from AFR listeners is from non-Orthodox who are seeking Orthodoxy. So, figuring some of these will be of interest to some of you, I've decided to share some email exchanges I've had with AFR listeners.

Dear Fr. Joseph,

Last week I finally decided to visit an Orthodox church. You know what? I couldn't understand a word they were saying. What gives?

Confused in Carolina

Dear Confused,

Look, if we made it too easy for folks to join in, everyone would want to be Orthodox! We just couldn't handle all of that at one time.

One day at a time. Hope this helps.

Fr. Joseph

Dear Fr. Joseph,

I'm thinking of joining the Orthodox Church. Which jurisdiction should I join?

Sincerely seeking,

Jan

Dear Jan,

Well, here's the deal: that movie, *My Big Fat Greek Wedding*—everyone who's Greek knows that's really a *documentary!* So be prepared.

If you like potato pancakes, can you spell *pierogi*? And, if you enjoy totally unpronounceable names, I would suggest joining the Orthodox Church in America (OCA).

Those who are accomplished in math, particularly subtracting thirteen days from any date on the calendar, might want to consider joining the Serbs or the Russian Orthodox Church Outside of Russia (ROCOR). But be careful—you know how that old Army song goes (and I paraphrase):

> *We're in the Synod now . . .*
> *No one's allowed to smile.*

When my family moved from the Russian Church Abroad back to the Antiochian Archdiocese, my then eight-year-old daughter asked, "Dad, what will be different?"

I said, "Well, essentially, nothing. But at certain parties and conferences we might encounter cultural things like, oh—belly dancing."

About five minutes later I asked, "Do you know what belly dancing is?"

She said, "Hmm . . . dancing on your belly, I guess!"

Anyway, some folks think that when you join the Antiochians, you're given an icon and a hula-hoop. That's completely false. Believe me—you have to *pay* for the hula-hoop!

There are smaller legitimate groups in America, like the Bulgarians and Romanians, but beware of any group calling themselves Orthodox who have a book bigger than a computer manual, or a four-hour website read, that explains their pedigree and just how really, really *real* they are.

They're just faking.

Hope this helps,

Fr. Joseph

———

Fr. Joseph,

Ever since my husband heard your podcast about St. Elvis he's been tormenting our family with his singing, shaking, and snarling. He's also demanding fried PB&J sandwiches on fast days.

Can you help me?

Susie in Alabama

PS—Some say I look like Ann-Margret. Is there hope for me, too?

Dear Susie,

First off, there is a St. Anne and there are even saints with names that translate to Margaret. Yet none of them ever starred in an Elvis movie.

Tell your husband not to get "All Shook Up" about it. I never said Elvis *Presley* was a saint. Then again, I never said your husband wasn't.

Sincerely,

Fr. Joseph

———

Dear Fr. Joseph,

I understand there are rules against priests dancing, and rules against priests swimming in public. It would help me greatly if you would point me to a rule forbidding priests singing in the shower.

Sincerely,

Matushka Xenobia

———

Dear Matushka,

Please be in contact with Susie from Alabama.

Fr. Joseph

Y'all, seriously, whatever our backgrounds, there's much that we understand about each other. However, there's a lot that gets lost in translation. It's one thing for American converts to adopt new recipes, foreign phrases, and customs; it's another for cradles to understand where the converts are coming from and why. It's another thing entirely when converts start speaking with a foreign accent! And the clergy who must shepherd this colorful flock? God help them!

Orthodoxy in America is still a long way from an *American* Orthodoxy. A "cradle" Orthodox Christian, Fr. Aris Metrakos, once published an article entitled, "There is an American Orthodoxy." Here are a few quotes:

> A myth needs to be debunked. It goes like this: Orthodox unity is years away because there is no such thing as "American Orthodoxy." Call it an ecclesiastical instead of urban legend if you want. It's been in circulation for at least two decades among the Orthodox Christians of the United States and it keeps us frozen in a state of tribalism and territorialism that prevents us from planting Orthodoxy more firmly in America.
>
> This myth is advanced by people who focus on what the Church in the United States is not. OK, so we don't have a 1500-year-old monastic tradition. It's also true that most of our people have never been to a vigil. And yes, the typical American churchgoer doesn't know Seraphim Rose from Pete Rose.
>
> But to say that these "shortcomings" imply that there is no American Orthodox identity is like saying there is no

such thing as American soccer because our fans don't pummel one another and our announcers don't scream "G-O-O-O-A-A-L!"

And he goes on:

I'm a patriot, but I'll admit that Americans can suffer from hubris. American Orthodox Christians are drowning in it. Most of us know it all—just ask us!

A choir member of forty years laughs openly at a priest that tries to explain what the "first tone" is, not realizing that if she had even the smallest grasp of the relationship between the notes in the ecclesiastical modes, it would take her choir just ten minutes instead of an hour to learn a simple hymn.

A longtime member of the Ladies' group stands up at a meeting and asks, "Where the h--- did Father come up with this fast before Christmas?"

A Sunday School teacher fails to take advantage of a seminar offered at a neighboring parish because she "already knows it all."

A businessman is asked to run for Parish Council because "he has so much to offer the Church" even though he attends Liturgy sporadically, doesn't participate in the sacraments, has no consistent prayer life, and doesn't give sacrificially.

Knowing that you don't know much is a sign of maturity. Do we want to move from adolescence into adulthood? Then we need to swallow our pride and admit that the first step in acquiring an adult faith is authentically uttering, "I don't know."

Yes, well, there it is.

But we're getting there—one generation, one day, and one step at a time. If the Church in America, much like her members, knows one thing, it's this: Fall down, get back up, fall down, get back up; Orthodoxy is slow, and thank God for that! In the meantime, we work together and hope to one day really, really *be* together. After all, think about it:

> If you could become Orthodox like a Romanian,
> Experience it like a Serbian,
> Be loyal to it like a Ukrainian,
> Sacrifice for it like a Russian,
> Be proud of it like an Arab,
> And enjoy it like a Greek,
> What a great faith you'd have,
> Especially if in addition you got to call yourself
> an *American*.

In the meantime, don't be surprised if sometimes, in the Church in America, the honest answer is simply, "I don't know."

The Great Orthodox Awakening

I was on my way to a seminar, having spent the night in a coffeehouse. Did you know that ever since the Orthodox Church bought out Starbuck's, they now have overnight rooms available? Yep.

Then the Orthodox Media limo arrived sporting a big Blockbuster ad on its trunk with endorsements of various movies by popular monks, priests, and bishops. There I was, being whisked away to a meeting of MMPFACF—the Media-Minded People for the Furtherance of the Ancient Christian Faith.

We had to speed, clipping a hundred miles per hour most of the way, to try to stay away from the ecclesiastical paparazzi. You know how it is whenever there's an Orthodox gathering these days.

The Great American Orthodox Hall had the red carpet rolled out, from entryway to curb. But, to keep it all in perspective, the word "HUMILITY" was embossed in large white letters down the center of the runner.

As the limo pulled up curbside, the gathered choir of 5,000 voices began to sing "Eis Polla eti Despota," only to stop when the door was opened to reveal it was just me, one of thousands of Orthodox podcasters. The choir not only shut up, they shifted their gaze to the car behind us, hoping to open their mouths and once again sing "Many Years," this time to a bishop. It was hard to get out of the big black people-mover—what with one hand cuffed to the briefcase I had been given by the mysterious man during last night's secret rendezvous (but more on that later).

I understood my mission. With Orthodoxy having become so popular, so suddenly, now was the time to really excite the masses and generate much-needed revenue for all the parishes. After all those years of struggle—little apartment missions, garage cathedrals and such—here we were entering a new era, thanks to what many were calling the Great Orthodox Awakening.

Some say it all started when Bill Gates admitted that the term *icons*, which represents windows into heaven—and thus, *Windows*—is really trademarked by the Orthodox Church. Not to mention when Steve Jobs and others finally came clean about that Apple design going back thousands of years to the very Genesis of man. Yep, after those two saw the light, the money really started rolling in.

Now some of our churches have icon screens that offer flat-panel LED displays of saints; you can even change them from time to time with software and downloads. Since they are lighted like a TV image, there's no need for all those candles. It also didn't hurt when Tom Hanks began promoting his newfound faith, the Steelers started wearing three-bar crosses on their helmets, and Taco Bell started boasting of its Wednesday, Friday, and fasting menus.

Then there was Jeremiah Riddle, who owned an old bubblegum factory. His was the bright idea to produce saints cards, like they used to do with baseball cards, and stick one in each pack of bubblegum. Now that idea took off like hotcakes! Ever had rosewater-flavored gum? Not bad!

Speaking of hotcakes: Syrup sales have gone downhill since replacing Aunt Jemima with St. Jemima, but marketing folks think finding a plumper saint (hence a bigger bottle) will help. As they say, "It's all in the name," and St. Thecla peanut butter is doing well. It's been crazy.

Then, as I mentioned earlier, there was this attaché case chained to my left wrist. Now that was weird. This guy walked right up to me in the ODS—you know, the Orthodox Dollar Store, where they sell paper icons, holy water bottles, single carnations, cheap charcoal, incense, and, of course, Jeremiah Riddle's bubblegum and trading cards. Anyway, the guy who gave me the briefcase was quiet, humble, and determined. As he handed it to me, I was mesmerized by his eyes. He'd clipped the cuffs around my wrist and said, "Don't open till your meeting. You'll know when the time is right."

Just as I was remembering the stranger's words, something peculiar happened: with a Tarzan yell, in came Ted. Ted's a recent convert to Orthodoxy, and he's certainly one of the more exotic members of our media committee. Since converting to Orthodoxy, Ted's forgone the old razor (and some say bathing) and always makes a grand entrance. Today, he's apparently Tarzan.

"Hey, Ted," Frank says, "how 'bout doing that in tone one?"

"Russian or Byzantine?" asks Ted. Then, just as we're grimacing politely, in walks our Art & Design chairman. He's a cradle Orthodox who'd always gone by the name "Terry" until last year, when he visited a monastery. Now he's Eleftherios. He has become smitten with anything having to do with iconography. He, too, does a little song the way the Greeks sing, "Kyrie eleison, Kyrie eleison." It rhymes: "Care to see some icons . . . Care to see some icons . . . Care to see some icons?"

Having been so anxious to present the contents of the mysterious briefcase, I suddenly realized I had been first to enter the room. And now, who should appear but Brother Dave: "Hello, gentlemen, it's good to see you today. The weather is nice—87 degrees, low humidity, and only a 25 percent chance of showers—low tonight in the mid-50s."

Brother Dave works in radio. He's always up-to-date on the weather, news, and latest market reports. He's supposed to present a new set of radio ads at this week's meeting, which caused me to pause. So much has happened so rapidly since *everyone* started catching onto Orthodoxy. For example, Oprah, Dr. Phil—even Talk Radio—all those shows fell out of favor among the masses, not so much due to conversion as to confession. Seems that once folks started availing themselves of the Sacrament of Confession, they weren't as outraged, they weren't as needy, and they especially didn't want to hear about everyone else's problems all the time. *That* was a good thing.

But not everything was good. There was last week's suggested Orthodox Radio commercial; if I remember correctly, it went something like a monster truck ad: "SUNDAY! SUNDAY! SUNDAY!"

We all said, "Unh-uh."

That's when Brother Dave went all retro on us, ripping off a seventies Coke ad: "I'd like to teach the world tone five, in perfect harmony . . ."

"NO!" We cried.

"How 'bout this one," he said (á la Alka Seltzer): "I can't believe I stood the whole time!"

"Not a chance."

"Or," he continued (sticking with seventies TV ads): "Orthodoxy. Try it. You'll like it!"

"Absolutely not," we moaned.

That was our last session together. Now, this week, with the full membership assembled, our chairman Frank called the meeting to order with a familiar prayer: "Dear God, we thank You that we are not like other men. Amen!"

Though it made me nervous, we laughed. That's when I thought of the attaché case handcuffed to my wrist and thought surely this must be the moment, the moment the stranger had mentioned, when I would know it was time to open the briefcase.

So, dear reader, what do you think was inside that briefcase? Was it full of money—and finally Orthodoxy was on its way? No. How about the other direction? Was the briefcase full of dust to remind us that we are but dust and to dust we shall return? Nope.

No doubt some of you might have thought it contained a pearl, reminding us of the pearl of great price that is the Holy Church. Or maybe it was a simple little slip of paper with the word "LOVE" or "HUMILITY" written on it?

Well, those are all good answers, but the way I remember it, it was none of these. Rather, all of us Orthodox media and marketing hotshots gathered around the mysterious attaché case and opened it only to find a photo album, sepia-toned and venerable-looking. We leafed through the pages and viewed the photos—old photos, not icons—of those who had gone before:

- ➤ Martyrs who refused to bow to the heresy of Islam.

- ➤ Mothers who died concealing the whereabouts of their children, by which the Faith was preserved.

- ➤ Immigrants—poor and hearty—bringing the Ancient Faith to a new land.

- ➤ Women—Syrian, Slav, Lebanese, Palestinian, and Greek—working endless hours cooking, sewing, and cleaning to pay the bills of fledgling church communities.

- ➤ Or in funeral attire, burying faithful forebears.

- ➤ Even faithful Russians being persecuted by the godless authorities.

- ➤ And simple pictures of solemn men, women, and children at prayer in their icon corners.

Needless to say, we were all ashamed of our grand schemes, incorporating secular corporate America into our evangelistic plans. We all agreed. We prayed. We cried. We repented. We vowed, then and there, to get back to the work of salvation.

Brother Dave, the radio guy? Well, he just couldn't stop himself—he just had to share with us one last radio ad idea (á la the old McDonald's jingle): "Two all-night vigils, special cloths, lettuce pray, please, icicles on a Slavic-shaped dome!"

"No!" we shouted.

In the end, it all goes back to what St. Seraphim said: "Acquire the Holy Spirit, and thousands around you will be saved."

Hello Jiddo, Hello Yaya

Growing up, I went to church camp on the coast, North Carolina Baptist Assembly at Fort Caswell, by the Oak Island Lighthouse. I especially remember the lighthouse because, my first year at camp, it kept me awake at night.

There's a back story there. Once, I forget how young I was, I guess my dad was a little put out with my mom. That night found us outside together, and up in the sky was one of those searchlight things used to sweep the evening sky to alert you to the county fair, a new restaurant, or a new place of entertainment.

I said, "Dad, what's that?"

He said, "Oh, that? That's a mama-eater."

"What?" I asked.

"A mama-eater," he said.

I don't recall what I thought about that at the time, but I was old enough, smart enough, to know that light sweeping the sky had never eaten anybody. I mean—*right?*

Anyway, back to camp and that lighthouse: Like clockwork that light came sweeping past my bunk bed window, again and again, and, of course, I thought of my mom. My first year at camp I'd have probably thought of Mom regardless, but thanks to dear ol' Dad and that lighthouse, the memory remains poignant.

I also remember the thrill of being away from home and being a kid among kids, even if we did have to go to church services a lot. I found I actually enjoyed the worship, without Mom and Dad being there. I do believe that my faith was strengthened, year after year,

35

by that adolescent experience. As I grew older, I kept going to church camps, as a youth director and a priest.

In many respects, church camp is church camp, and really, for kids and parents, the fears and fun of camping are fairly universal: camp is camp. The following letter's author remains anonymous; it's funny because it represents every parent's fears:

Dear Mom & Dad,

Our cabin leader told us to write to our parents in case you saw the flood on TV and are worried. We are okay. Only one of our tents and two sleeping bags got washed away. Luckily, none of us got drowned because we were all up on the mountain looking for Adam when it happened. Oh yes, please call Adam's mother and tell her he is okay. He can't write because of the cast.

I got to ride in one of the search and rescue jeeps. It was neat. We never would have found Adam in the dark if it hadn't been for the lightning.

Our cabin leader got mad at Adam for going on a hike alone without telling anyone. Adam said he did tell him, but it was during the fire so he probably didn't hear him. Did you know that if you put gas on a fire, the gas will blow up? The wet wood didn't burn, but one of the tents did and also some of our clothes. Matthew is going to look weird until his hair grows back.

We will be home on Saturday if our camp director gets the bus fixed. It wasn't her fault about the wreck. The brakes worked okay when we left for our field trip. The camp director said that with a bus that old, you have to expect something to break down; that's probably why she can't get insurance. We think it's a neat bus. She doesn't care if we get it dirty, and if it's hot, sometimes she lets us ride on the fenders. It gets pretty hot with 45 people in a bus. She let us take turns riding in the trailer until the highway patrol man stopped and talked to us.

The camp director is a neat lady. Don't worry, she's a good driver. In fact, she is teaching Jesse how to drive on the mountain roads where there isn't any traffic. All we ever see up there are logging trucks.

This morning all of the kids were diving off the rocks and swimming out in the lake. My cabin leader wouldn't let me because I can't swim, and Adam was afraid he would sink because of his cast, so he let us take the canoe across the lake. It was great. You can still see some of the trees under the water from the flood. Our cabin leader isn't crabby like some of them. He didn't even get mad about us not wearing lifejackets.

Josie and I threw up, but the cook said it probably was just food poisoning from the leftover chicken. She said they got sick that way with food they ate in prison.

I have to go now. We are going to town to mail our letters and buy some more candy and fireworks. Don't worry about anything. We are fine.

Love,

George

P.S. How long has it been since I had a tetanus shot?

Heh!

But for those parents who feel that impending kid-separation anxiety brought on by the advent of church camp: relax. It'll be okay. You won't receive a letter like that any more because, really, who writes letters any more?

Yet, just for fun, I did. While online, I found one of these fun sites where all you have to do is list some nouns, verbs, and adjectives, then click a button and *voila*, instant Official Camp Letter! I don't know why (maybe because he'd just celebrated twenty-five years as bishop), but I chose His Grace, Bishop Antoun. I entered his name, my name, and the words *sorta, ugly, communion, tailgate, lie, swore, tired, hairy, stole, slippery, swim,* and *confession.* Here's what I got:

An Official Camp Newsletter

Dear <u>Bishop Antoun</u>,
Camp is <u>ugly</u> and <u>hairy</u>.
I am <u>sorta</u> like it.
I have learned to <u>swim</u> the camp's <u>communion</u>.
The weather is really <u>slippery</u>.
I hope to <u>lie</u> in the camp's <u>tailgate</u> tomorrow.
Please!—<u>swore</u> my <u>tired</u> saint.
Love, Fr. Joseph Huneycutt

P.S. I <u>stole</u> your <u>shiny</u> <u>confession</u>!

The more I thought about it, the more I liked it. In fact, His Grace may like it, too. I may just send it!

There's a famous song parody by Allan Sherman from way back in the sixties called "Hello Muddah, Hello Fadduh." You've probably heard it before, but here's an Orthodox camp version (which may be sung to the same tune):

Hello Jiddo, hello Yaya.
Here I am at Camp for Martyrs.
Camp is very entertaining
And they say we'll even study icon painting.

I share my bunk with Joseph Spivey.
He snores just like Amou and Tye-tee.
Next you see me, I'll be thinner—
They serve rice and lentils every night for dinner.

All the couns'lors hate the waiters,
I swear the girls are instigators,
And the priest, he wants no sissies,
So he reads to us from John Climacus-isis.

Now I don't want this should scare ya,
See, my counselor, he's from Bulgaria.

He reminds me of Uncle Marty—
Gosh, they really both sure know just how to party.

I'll be home soon, oh Jiddo, Yaya,
They won't keep me, cuz I'm no martyr!
Don't fret 'cause I have not been there
But I am halfway through that book by Timothy Ware!

When I'm home, I promise I will not make noise,
Or mess the house with all my toys.
Believe me, it's no jest,
I'm gonna become a hairy hesychast.

Tell my father, and my mother,
tell my sister and my brother,
I will come home, I know they miss me,
Guess what—I can swing a censer like a Frisbee.

Wait a minute, someone's yelling,
Seems it's time now for confessing.
Tying prayer ropes or chanting tone five,
Jiddo, Yaya, camp is one fun holy wild ride!

Anyway, when the time for registering for the various Orthodox summer camps comes around: *Do it!* Parents, I cannot tell you how beneficial it is for your sons and daughters to be around Orthodox kids from all over the country in the spiritually forming environs of church camp. No matter the cost, it's worth every penny. There's usually some sort of help available for those who need it; ask. But do not, *do not*, delay in registering. Camp is a big, BIG deal for the kids, and the slots fill quickly. (Orthodox Christians may come late to church, but they register early for camp!)

Besides, depending on where you live, you just never know when you might see one of those mama-eaters in the sky. I don't think they're a menace, but let's not find out! Be prepared! Register your kids for Orthodox church camp! You'll be glad—blessed—you did.

Orthodox Christian Anarchist at Large

A while back, I met an honest-to-goodness Orthodox Christian anarchist. I'd bought a newspaper in hopes of solving the crossword puzzle and scanning the comics. I was leafing through the other sections when, in the classifieds, I found the following job listing: *OCAL: Orthodox Christian Anarchist at Large seeks willing accomplices.*

This was followed by an 800 number, stating that there were representatives available in all areas. "What the heck is an Orthodox Christian Anarchist?" I wondered. Curious, I called the number.

"You have reached the worldwide headquarters of Christian Anarchy. If you are Protestant, press one; Roman Catholic, press two; Orthodox, press three . . ."

So I pressed three.

"Welcome to Orthodox Christian Anarchy. Please leave your name and phone number and one of our representatives will return your call."

I lied—I said my name was "Curtis" and gave them the church phone number, and then I hung up. I probably shouldn't have done it. After a few days, I forgot all about it.

A week or so later I entered the church office just in time to hear the secretary saying, "Sir, I've told you three times already and I'll tell you again: We do not have a Curtis here!"

I stood staring at her, paralyzed. I motioned for her to put him on hold. I said, "Oops, he may be looking for me, it's a long story. See if he'll give you a local return number, street address or something."

She did and he did, and then, well, I didn't know what to do. I watched as she scribbled down a street address—oh my. Curiosity got the best of me and, long story short, I dressed down to shorts, a sport shirt, Birkenstocks, and dark glasses, and headed over to 666 Wayward Drive.

I pulled up in front of a nondescript storefront office. Over the door was a big sign that read, "RUMOR." As I approached the tinted glass door I saw the inscription: "Al Zeebop, OCAL—Orthodox Christian Anarchist at Large."

As I entered the cacophony of chaos, the noise was almost maddening; then—*ding-dong* blared the door chime. A man emerged from a side room, closed the door, and the sounds were muffled; then silence.

"Greetings!" he said.

This man looked so very familiar, not really like a parishioner—but I dunno. It could be I'd seen him in a church before, but I wasn't sure which church. Regardless, I was going to play it safe and, hopefully, remain incognito.

"Welcome to Orthodox Christian Anarchy!" he said. "Pardon the noise, rehearsals, you know. Say, you look familiar. Have I seen you before?"

"Probably not," I lied. "I'm new to the area."

"Great," he said. "Newcomers are the best in the business, if you know what I mean!"

He winked at me. I didn't know what he meant and wasn't sure I wanted to. He had me sit down across a desk from him. He pulled out a briefcase, opened it up, and inside were various vials of different colors.

He said, "These are the tools of the trade, the *Humors*, if you will. But around here we just refer to them as *Rumors*." Again, a wink.

I was starting to feel uncomfortable. This guy didn't know me from Adam, and here he was sharing seemingly inside stuff without asking for personal info, credentials, anything. Then I heard a great moaning sound from down the hallway. Mr. Zeebop (I guessed that was his name) said, "Excuse me a sec." As he disappeared down the narrow hallway, I couldn't be sure, but it appeared that he entered a room where a man was chained to the wall as in some medieval dungeon.

I glanced at the other doors and noticed they were labeled. The one my host had entered was labeled "Sweet Dreams." There were other doors: one labeled "Whispers," another labeled "Flattery." It was just then that Mr. Zeebop exited the "Sweet Dreams" room; again I thought I saw a man chained to the wall, and Zeebop came back to the desk smiling.

"So, what do you think, Mr.—uh—?"

"Curtis," I said. "Just call me Curtis. And what should I call you?" I asked.

"You know, my friends just call me Bubba. My first name actually starts with a 'B'—it's a big ol' long name, seldom heard in these parts, and using the initial 'B' in front of my name often makes folks ill at ease. So, I just go by 'Bubba'." (Honestly, I had no idea what he was talking about: *B. Al Zeebop, Bubba*.)

"What does the 'B' actually stand for?" I asked.

"BOO!" he said, and laughed.

We were then interrupted by someone leaving the "Whispers" room. As he passed by me, I could barely make out some words or phrases:

All he cares about is money . . .
He's a hypocrite . . .
Homosexual . . .
Adulterer . . .
Breaks the seal of confession . . .

"Tony!" said Mr. B—I mean Bubba. "Tony, have you met Curtis?"

"No. Pleased to meet you, Curtis. What church do you attend?" he said.

"I'm new to the area, so I haven't settled yet," I said.

"Oh, you want to be careful of that Fr. Titus," Tony whispered.

"There's some stories going around about him." (I couldn't catch the last things the man said because we were suddenly interrupted by more moaning coming from the back of the hall.)

"What is that sound?" I asked.

"Oh, *heh heh*, that's poor ol' Fr. Titus now," my host replied.

"You have him locked up—chained to the wall?" I asked.

"Well, not exactly," Tony said. "That's like a specter of him—a hologram of sorts, representing Fr. Titus's emotional state these days, since the beginning of the campaign—which has been very successful, I might add."

I thought he was full of beans, but I acted interested nonetheless. As Tony the Whisperer exited the building, Mr. B, er, Beebop—or whatever—said, "Let me give you a tour, Curtis."

The first room we entered was the one Tony had just left, the one labeled "Whispers." There were all sorts of folks milling about whispering gossip and rumors, half-truths and innuendos.

From there we went down the hall and into the room labeled "Flattery." These people wore some of the widest grins, gave big hugs, and acted like I was the greatest thing to have ever walked through that door. They complimented me and sang my praises until we got outside the door.

After Bubba had closed the door, he said, "Now listen." I put my ear up to the wood, only to hear them saying all manner of bad things about me, most of them untrue.

Finally, we approached the room where I thought I'd seen a man chained to the wall. It was labeled "Sweet Dreams." We stood outside this room and Bubba said, "I'm sorry, I cannot take you into this room. It would be too great of a burden for you."

From where we stood I could hear the man inside moaning; yet we turned and headed back toward Bubba's desk.

"What are the vials for?" I asked.

He said he'd actually stolen the vials from the Enemy. They contained various elixirs to aid in forgetfulness.

"Forgetfulness?" I asked.

"Yes," he said, "when used properly—by the Enemy, that is—the fumes emanating from these bottles help the clergy to forget all words spoken in malice, all deeds done out of envy and spite. Basically, in the service of the Enemy, those who inhale these aromas are likened unto their Leader, who on the Cross said, 'Father, forgive them, for they know not what they do.'"

"Okay, so what do you anarchists or antagonists, or whatever you are, what do you use them for? I mean, what do they help your minions to forget?"

"That they're Christian, *heh heh*," he said. "It is so simple. If we can get Christians to forget Christ, well, the Church can be such a fun place for us. If you get my drift."

Just then a call came in on Mr. B's cell. As he listened to the caller, his face turned red. He snapped his phone shut abruptly and said, "I'm sorry, I have to go. One of our top agents is currently headed toward confession. If I get there in time, we may be able to use the occasion to our advantage. Do you have any other questions, Mr. uh—?"

"Curtis," I said. "Yes, I do. Who were those awful singers I heard upon entering?"

"Ah yes!" he exclaimed: "The Stereotypes. This is one of our greatest tools—it keeps certain people *out* of the Church, if you get my drift. We've got Asians and African-Americans just hanging out here with nothing better to do. The people in the Church, thanks to our vapors and hard work, haven't seemed to notice a need to convert them or to welcome them into their parishes."

"Stereotypes? But what about Hispanics?" I said. "They're sorely lacking in the Church, too."

"Oh, we've got 'em: Julio, Hor-hay, Hernandez?!"

"*Si, Señor!*"

"See," he said, "they're over there just napping in the corner."

As my evil host was speaking, my fingers edged ever closer to those vials of forgetfulness. I wasn't sure what I was going to do, but I knew I had to do something.

"You know," he said, "we used to have a lot of white folks hang-ing out with the Stereotypes. But, thanks to their being welcomed more and more into the churches, we have trained them well—a little bit of the *Rudder*, legalism, judgmentalism, fundamentalism, etc., goes a long way with Caucasian converts. Someday, and I hope it never comes, we may have to train up the Asians, Blacks, and His-panics to wreak havoc in the churches. But, for now, they're a lot better off just hanging out here playing stereotypes."

Quickly I thrust a vial under Bubba's nose and said, "Sorry about this, Mr. B, but you never saw me. I'm not even here." And with that I ran past him and entered the room with the moaning man.

But he wasn't there. In fact, no one was there. Instead, I found myself back outside, in the parking lot. Well, that was even better! I hastened to my car and sped away, setting the GPS to Fr. Titus's church. I needed to find out what was going on.

Fr. Titus sat behind his desk. He was reading a book called *Antag-onists in the Church*, and he looked much better than his holographic image I'd seen imprisoned over at Orthodox Christian Anarchists. He said, "Sit down, Fr. Joseph; I want to read you something. Listen to this:

> Antagonism can obliterate a sense of the presence of God's love in individuals and in the faith community. It is an affliction of the whole people of God. Perhaps antagonism most frequently tears into the lives of church staff mem-bers.
>
> Those who lavish effusive, gushing praise on you now will often be equally generous with criticism later. . . . What causes this shift? One possibility may be unrealis-tic expectations. To be human is to have faults. You cannot sustain the level of perfection that antagonists expect. (It is also possible that they become jealous of the image they have built up for you and consequently seek to destroy it by bringing you down to size. In any case, beware of someone

who heaps excessive praise on you. This person is waving a
red flag.)

"It has been said," I interjected, "Once a priest-hater, always a
priest-hater."

Fr. Titus agreed, and then continued reading a list of reasons
folks might follow an antagonist:

- ➤ People sometimes mistake antagonists for activists.
- ➤ The truth is often far less exciting than lies and half-truths.
- ➤ Bad news is more exciting than good news.
- ➤ Some people are gullible, and antagonists take advantage
  of that.
- ➤ Some people tend to follow orders without question.
- ➤ Some people are intimidated by antagonists.
- ➤ Many persons just don't want to rock the boat.
- ➤ People follow antagonists to be one of the crowd.
- ➤ Some join antagonists as a way to express their own
  feelings.
- ➤ Others follow antagonists because of misguided loyalties.
- ➤ Some follow antagonists because antagonists frequently
  make their followers feel important.

"What do you think of that?" he asked.

I said, "The priest is often not recognized unless he is on the
cross. And in some communities there's always one—or a handful—
that will try to make sure he stays there. Yet these folks need salvation, too, Father. I mean, as pastors, we still have to minister to the
antagonists. Believe me, it's not easy. As one priest told me, 'There
are people who are so needy, who have so many problems, they think
only the priest can fix them. And when that priest doesn't have all
the answers—God help that priest!'"

"*Heh heh*, boy, is that ever true! I've been suffering a lot lately,"
Fr. Titus said. "Until, all of a sudden, by the grace of God—I mean it

was like someone burst into my heart with a potion for forgetting! The fog cleared and I was able to get some relief."

I thought back to the vial of vapor that I'd stolen before entering the torture room. What had I done with that thing? Wait. Was it even real? I couldn't even remember the street address—66-something—and the man in charge: Al Zeebop, or Bubba, B. Al. Zeebop? I couldn't recall. The thing that stuck in my mind was: *Rumor.* I guess it was all just . . . a rumor.

Just then, Fr. Titus burst out laughing. He said, "I'll never forget, back in seminary, ol' Fr. George used to say: 'Sometimes at night, when I am saying my prayers, I end by saying, "God bless all the people that I don't like and all the people who don't like me." And that covers a mighty multitude.'"

What else could I say but "Amen."

Help! There's an Iconostasis in My Living Room!

Normally, I don't watch television; we don't subscribe to cable or satellite at our house. But on a recent road trip I found myself lying on a hotel bed holding the old clicker and getting very, very sleepy. You know how it is. *Tick, tock, tick, tock, tick, tock . . .*

You're getting very sleepy. Very. Very. Sleepy.

Anyway, I was dozing with one eye and surfing the channels with the other when I heard a great commotion. It was a woman squealing, "Oh my God! My Lord! Oh my God!" At that point I was thinking, "Yep, this is why we don't watch television: all that swearin' and stuff."

As she ranted into delirium, I realized it was one of those extreme home makeover shows. You know, where they take a perfectly normal-looking lived-in room and secretly make it over to look like a cubby in a dollhouse—full of pastels, stainless steel, art deco, fringe, and stripes. Then the "customer" returns home and acts like they have flat out lost their mind! They yelp something like, "Oh, adhao-ghua-Kognehoehgeoirgbnlk!"

Returning to my TV-induced hypnotic state, I was listening to this woman scream "God" and "Jesus" and such, when she suddenly blurted out, "There's an iconostasis in my living room!" And the camera panned over and, sure enough, the makeover crew had installed an icon screen in this couple's living room!

I sat up, staring at the TV. I mean, has Orthodoxy become so mainstreamed that they're now making television shows about mission work? I tried to change the channel, but the remote no longer worked; the TV show I was watching seemed stuck in a loop with the woman tearfully yelling "My God," and the camera kept panning over the room to show the newly installed icon of Christ on the iconostasis in the couple's living room.

That's when there came a knock at the door, but it wasn't an ordinary door knock. As dreams normally go, it was both a knock and a huge two-ton Russian church bell in the key of "F". I got up from the hotel room bed and headed toward the door. I looked through the peephole, only to see a whole crowd of people! Although the view was distorted by the fish-eye door hole thingy, I could tell from my experience with iconography that the whole hotel hallway—now the size of a coliseum—was filled with saints. They were easily identifiable, all wearing their "icon clothes" and stiff poses, with gold lights circling their heads.

There it was again, that door-knock-Russian-church-bell sound. I opened the door to see only one guy. He stood there, sans halo. In standard dream style, there wasn't really any dialogue; he just came into the room and sat down with his sales case. It was at that moment that—as often happens in dreams—I understood that he was there to make over my hotel room into a kind of Orthodox chapel.

He opened up his catalogue. Wow. I never realized there were so many Orthodox variations, or that you could do so much with a hotel room. He showed me my options.

There was what he called the Russian package, very beautiful with a big ol' iconostasis and more icons than any Greek would ever need. Yet it was one of the cheaper packages because there were no pews.

He moved on to the Greek room makeover. Aha! Marble! Lots of mosaics, pews, and—here's where it got pricey—there was even an organ! He paused a moment on a page that seemed out of place—really churchy, but not very Byzantine—I must have looked confused. He said, "Western Rite."

Though I was dreaming, I still knew my place: I wasn't rich. I said, "Show me the cheapest thing you've got." That's when he flipped to the back of the book and the plywood iconostasis with paper icons taped to it.

"Oh my goodness!" I cried. You see, I'd been there before.

Back when I was an Episcopalian on my way to Orthodoxy, I really weirded out the missus. Oh sure, she was ready to move on from where we were, but she was not one hundred percent on fire for Eastern Orthodoxy. (For some reason, Orthodoxy's funny that way, guys and gals.) I'd had a prayer desk, or *prie-dieu*, commissioned in seminary, and it was downstairs in my study. One day, while my wife was out shopping, I spirited the prayer desk upstairs and placed it in the living room with an icon above it and some prayer books on top. It was way too churchy for the rest of the furniture, but I thought, "Boy, will she be surprised!" (Ladies, you can imagine.)

Then, as we moved closer to our jump to Orthodoxy, we used to gather with a couple of friends from our current Episcopal church community and, under closed blinds and behind locked doors—are you ready for this? We would look at icon catalogues! Then, when we had a little extra cash, we'd order some icons, books, incense, and stuff; and when the mailman came—"Woo-hoo!" Extreme Orthodox Makeover!

Then it got even weirder. We eventually moved all the furniture out of a bedroom and moved the living room stuff in there. And I placed a desk, with a white bedsheet over it and some icons behind it, in the room that used to be a living room.

Later, I met with the local Greek priest and told him I wanted to convert to Orthodoxy and start an English-speaking Orthodox mission in the area. To my surprise, he said, "Great! The more the merrier!" He gave me a censer, censer stand, service books, icons, incense, charcoal, procession cross, and other makeover stuff—all of which went around that desk with the bed sheet, etc., in the former living room.

Now here comes the kicker: One of our fellows, who is now a monk on Mount Athos (but at the time he was a Baptist on his way to Byzantium)—this guy said, "What we really need is an iconostasis."

Y'all, this was a regular-sized room in a house that was about eighty years old. I'd guess the room was about, oh, 12 x 14 feet, and this guy wanted to build an iconostasis? He said, "I'll pay for it." I said, "Sure." The next Saturday, here he came driving his dad's truck with some top-grade plywood and a ladder on the back, toolbox, brackets and such. By late afternoon there was an iconostasis in my living room! Oh. My.

I felt like Richard Dreyfuss's character in *Close Encounters of the Third Kind*—you know, building a dirt mountain in his house. No doubt my wife started feeling a little like the woman with the extreme home makeover in my dream. Oh, I almost forgot to finish that story . . .

After the salesman had shown me the Russian room, Greek room, Western Rite room, and dirt-poor-convert plywood room, I looked back at the TV, back at him, and then, clicker in hand, I again tried to turn off the TV. Again, it wouldn't work. I kept pushing the button, pointing it at the TV, mashing & wiggling the remote. (You know how you do when the clicker's acting up.)

But then, in my dream, I noticed that it was no longer a TV clicker at all, but one of those holy water sprinklers, and every time I shook it toward changing the channel—water splashed on TV images. But wait. It wasn't a TV at all. It was an iconostasis! I turned toward the man with the sales kit. He was gone. In his place stood a choir of voices singing, "O Lord, save Thy people and bless Thine inheritance . . ."

I looked down at myself and saw I was vested; the floor was marble. Wow! I was in church. And images of all those saints I'd spotted while looking through the door's peephole were now adorning the walls and icon screen. The dream was so real that I started to actually believe I was awake.

And then, from over in the corner—swift and frightening—slithered a big black snake and a fire-breathing dragon, making their way toward me. Oh no . . . wha—? And then I spotted him: the sales guy from earlier, except now he was in a director's chair. I thought maybe he was directing my dream or something. Forgetting about the slithering creatures, with the choir continuing to sing "grant victory to Orthodox Christians over their adversaries," I made my way over to him and asked, "Are you directing this dream?"

"No," he said, "I'm directing the TV show you were watching. There seems to be some technical difficulty."

I asked, "Where am I?"

"You? Well, you're in your heart," he said. "You're in your heart, my friend. That's where the *real* makeover takes place." He pointed toward the nightstand, the hotel room nightstand, by the bed. (You know how dreams are: it was still the bedroom, but also the church—with a choir, a TV show director, an iconostasis and, but of course, snakes and dragons.) I thought he meant for me to open the drawer and pull out Gideon's Bible, and right at that moment, the choir broke into singing the Beatles' "Rocky Raccoon":

And now Rocky Raccoon, he fell back in his room
Only to find Gideon's Bible
Gideon checked out and he left it no doubt
To help with good Rocky's revival, ah . . .

And that's when—ain't this the way it always happens—things got so kooky in my dream that I woke up. Whew!

What, you may ask, did it all mean? Well, my best guess is this: Orthodoxy—salvation—is not all about the trimmings, the icons in the living room, vestments, and such. Rather, it's about the heart—the real living room where we meet the Lord. We meet the Lord in the heart. But first we have to continually make way for Him by clearing out all those snakes and dragons that lurk there!

All the other stuff simply serves to help get the job done.

The saints, that great cloud of witnesses, not only serve as our examples but, as St. Paul says, "They cheer us on to run the race"— circumcising the heart, clearing out the dragons that lurk there, making it a fitting place to meet the Lord.

Talk about extreme! Extreme *Heart* Makeover: *that's* what Orthodoxy's really all about.

Orthodox White Boy

Some of you may not understand this chapter. Why? Because I know for a fact there are folks reading this that are non-Orthodox: Baptists, Lutherans, Methodists, Anglicans, and, yes, even nominal Christians and secular types. Some people will definitely be offended. But I also suspect that some of those same people are, like me—come closer—white.

Here are some typical signs of Orthodox white people:

➤ *Have you written a book about your conversion to Orthodoxy?*
With the exception of Fr. James Bernstein, you are white.

➤ *Have you read a book about someone's conversion to Orthodoxy?*
No doubt, you are white.

➤ *What's that you say? You are an Orthodox blogger?*
Whitey, whitey, whitey.

➤ *What's that you say? You are an African-American convert?*
Yes, well, welcome to the club—and, in this club, you may as well be white, too.

By now there are some of you thinking, "Hey! You can't say things like that!" Well, I don't. But plenty of so-called ethnic Orthodox do. Ours is a community that worships, prays, teaches, and believes correctly, rightly: Orthodox. However, we've yet to get over a "party spirit" when it comes to our cultural and ethnic identities.

I was talking with a Serbian Orthodox priest once who was

making light of Serbian piety. He said that the Serbs don't always follow all the rules of piety, but they are really, really serious about remaining steadfastly Orthodox. He related the following tale:

> At a party one evening, various Orthodox fellows were arguing about which brand of Orthodoxy was the greatest. One guy exclaimed that it was obviously the Greeks.
>
> When asked, "Why do you say the Greeks?" he replied, "Oh my goodness; so much! I mean, there's the theology of the Church, the Church Fathers, the language of the New Testament, the Creed, and the very core of the Faith's theology. Of course the Greeks are the best!"
>
> Another man argued that it was surely the Russians. When asked to explain, he said, "Russians have given the Church beauty! Just look at all the beautiful Russian churches, the cathedrals, the vestments, the gold and the iconography. No doubt the Russians are the best!"
>
> That's when the Serb shouted, "Stop it! It is we Serbs who deserve the honor!"
>
> They all looked at him and said, "What have the Serbs offered Orthodoxy?"
>
> He replied, "Hmm. I don't know, but whatever it is, we're willing to die for it!"

Like the old joke about Baptists at the Pearly Gates, you could even have the white boy saying, "Well, how 'bout us?"

The cradles all look at him as if to say, "What on earth have you brought to the table?" and he replies, "My mom sent this casserole."

See? See how it is for Orthodox white folk? Think about this for a moment: No one ever asks a Greek, Arab, Russian, or Serb, "So, how did you come to Orthodoxy?"

For many American Orthodox converts, places like Bethlehem, Jerusalem, the Holy Sepulcher, and the River Jordan are mythical landmarks most often seen in the pages of a book. Yet I serve a church where a majority of the parishioners are *from* the Holy Land, even Bethlehem and Jerusalem. The Jordan River? It's in their backyard. How did *they* become Orthodox? Nuthin' to it!

Look, when folks ask me what I was before becoming Orthodox I always say, "Well, I grew up Baptist; in North Carolina that's a requirement." It's a joke, of course, but oftentimes it's just accepted as inevitable. It's like death and taxes. "Oh, North Carolina? Of course you're Baptist."

Orthodox white folks do the same. "Ah, you're from Serbia (Romania/Greece/Russia/Syria)—you must be Orthodox!" (Oh, I know, there are Muslims in those countries. But please, forgive me; this Muslim thing is new to most white folks. In other words, I'm not talking about them.)

I've got a felt cap that I often wear; not a clergy-type hat, but a secular one, a Kangol. I've had Greeks say to me, "Ah! That hat makes you look Greek!" And, no lie, I've had Russians say to me, "With that hat, you look Russian!" I figure what they're really saying is, "Wow, with that cap on, you don't look so much like a redneck."

Ever seen a white boy dancing the *dabkeh*? What's that? You have? Looked funny, didn't it? Ever seen a Russian belly dancer? Didn't think so. See what I mean?

Honest to goodness, I was once at a regional church affair, soon after becoming Orthodox, where the banquet was held in a local Lebanese restaurant. It was my first real taste of Arabic cuisine and loud, exotic Arabic music. Then—I am not making this up—there came a voice over the loudspeaker: "Ladies and gentlemen, please welcome the amazing Moo-stu-hah!" Look, having once been found in a Four Square Pentecostal church where I feared they were introducing a snake, I was anxious.

When I heard the announcement, given the affair I was experiencing, I thought, "Surely they're not going to have a belly dan—" Y'all? Yep! There she came. She was—there's really no way to put this without y'all thinking something bad—let me just say, the announcer was correct. She was amazing.

There I sat, a new priest (an Orthodox white boy, at that), wondering what I should do. After all, they don't have real live belly dancers in the Baptist Church; but I did grow up watching "I Dream of Jeanie." I looked around the dining hall and all the men, even clergy, and the women, were clapping and enjoying the performance. Not wanting to stand out like a big dub, I joined in, trying to act all un-Baptist.

Then suddenly one of the organizers of the event, Hella, came by and yelled, "Fr. Joseph! What are you doing? It's the art! Concentrate on the art!"

I thought to myself, "Oh no! What *was* I concentrating on?!" She was teasing me, of course. Orthodox white boys are easy targets in such settings.

By the way, did you know Russian clergy (ROCOR) are forbidden to use tobacco? Not that I'm advocating it, mind you, but Middle Eastern clergy do not have the same restrictions.

I once heard a priest tell a story of when he was in seminary at St. Vladimir's and the choir, the St. Vlad's Octet, was invited to perform at a Russian parish. This priest, then a seminarian, smoked. One of the professors told him, "Don't take your cigarettes; the Russians frown on that." This priest said, "Sure enough, at the banquet afterwards, no one smoked—but you couldn't get your elbows on the table for all the liquor bottles!"

I'm sure by now, there are some offended Orthodox white folks reading this—not to mention those Baptists! But don't be offended. At least not yet—there's more!

Let's go back to black folks; you guys, if you're Orthodox, get in line when visiting a different parish and see if they don't ask if you're Orthodox. The fact is—aside from Ethiopians, Somalis, and the occasional convert—there just ain't no black folks in the American Orthodox Church.

Oh, and don't any of you bigots think this is a haven for you and your twisted ideas. We've got enough to deal with! And be forewarned, each ethnic group, including your own, is just plain nutty,

nutty, **nutty**. Truth be known, until recently, the people an Anglo bigot would consider kosher (i.e., white)—they weren't to be found in many Orthodox churches either.

However, in the Orthodox Church, we have our own struggles with prejudice and profiling. I do it myself. In a large parish setting, with hundreds of people receiving Communion, I am more prone to commune without questioning folks who look Middle Eastern or Russian than I am those who look like Cracker Barrel. It's just true!

Back in the late eighties, after the mass conversions of the evangelicals, it is said that one of the official publications of the Antiochian Archdiocese ran a report about summer camp, saying, "There were even a lot of white people there!" Can you imagine? White folks are a minority in the Orthodox Church. And don't even look for demographic bars on blacks, Hispanics, and Asians.

So it's no wonder that many white folk converts have to go to extreme measures to prove their Orthodoxy. After all, you rarely see American Arab youth running around with 300-knot prayer ropes tied to their belt loops. Ever see many American Greek boys growing long beards and ponytails? How 'bout skipping showers, wearing Birkenstocks or icon lapel pins?

Orthodox white folk are more prone to fall prey to the trappings. No, I am not demeaning these things. If they help you toward the Kingdom, God bless you! (Except, that is, for not bathing. As my spiritual father used to say, "B.O. does not glorify God.") I'm just saying: The fact that Greeks, Arabs, Serbs, and Russians might not buy so many Orthodox thingies does not necessarily make them any less Orthodox.

Then there's the whole food thing. Orthodox white folks have to learn all the new dishes and names of food or drink.

Baklava or batlowah
Hummus or hoomas
Kvass and Stoli

Kibbeh, souvlaki, kulich
Baba ganoush, mahmool

Cradle Orthodox come to our house and have to learn:

Hot dog
Ham - burger
Buh - naa - nuh

But that's silly, of course, because they already know these!

So, what do white folks bring to the Orthodox table? The same as everyone else: souls seeking salvation. And, at least the way I understand it, souls ain't got no color, ethnicity, or culture.

Please, Greeks, listen up: *Culture* will not save you. Arabs: *Food* will not save you. Russians: *Vodka* will not save you. This is where all the Protestant readers are thinking, "Preach it, brother! Preach it!" Okay, here goes: *Protestantism* ain't gonna save you either! Only love saves. Only. Love. Saves.

I've often encountered a stranger at the chalice on a Sunday or big feast, and I've asked, "Are you Orthodox?"

To which has come the reply, "I'm from Syria!"

At the Last Day, our Lord is not going to ask, "Where are you from?"

At the Last Day, our Lord is not going to ask, "You Gr'ick?"

At the Last Day, our Lord is not going to ask, "Pravoslavni?"

At the Last Day, our Lord is not going to ask, "Do you like vinegar-flavored pork BBQ or the sweet red sauce?

(Though if He does, the correct answer is "vinegar.")

Red or yellow, black or white: Our Lord will ask, "Have you loved others as I have loved you?" (And, last I checked, that means every-body's welcome.)

It is on this standard that we shall be judged. Don't take it from me; I'm just an Orthodox white boy. Take it from the Scriptures and the witness of the saints. In other words, take it from the Church;

and you Baptists, Anglicans, Methodists, Lutherans, and nominal Christian mutts—oh, what the heck—you Jews and Muslims! Y'all come on over and convert, too! Y'all come on home to the True Faith. We'll make room! (Listen up, guys: We *will* make room, won't we? I mean—the Faith is universal, and the call is to *all*. Right?)

Hah! Oh, don't worry. I'm just kiddin'! Truth is, we ain't ready yet. But, little by little, we're gettin' there.

(I mean, shouldn't we be?)

Part II

A Little Feasting,
A Lot of Fasting

Fasters Anonymous

So there it was, the second week of the Great Fast of Lent, 2008. Week one—gone! Oh, I know, fasting is supposed to be in secret and all, but I've got to tell you something. Please don't tell anyone: I ended up attending my first meeting of Fasters Anonymous. It's a Twelve Step group that meets in the basement of a local Catholic church. That year, since Orthodox Easter was way later than the Catholics—and everyone else, for that matter—the group had already been meeting for five weeks. Yet, given my circumstances, I had to go.

And, jumping ahead in my tale a bit, do you know how this Twelve Step meeting ended? Unlike other Twelve Step programs where you pray the first portion of Reinhold Niebuhr's "Serenity Prayer," this group sang a fasting song to the tune of the *Gilligan's Island* theme song—at the beginning and the end! But more on that later.

As is my practice, my plan was to eat nothing—nothing, I say— from Sunday evening through Wednesday. That's a traditional way to enter the first week of the Great Fast of Lent: no food, at all, until after the Presanctified Liturgy on Wednesday. Believe me, it can be done. Anyway, that was my plan.

Monday? All day? No problem. Then came Tuesday. On Tuesday mornings our parish has adult Bible study. We'd been working on the Gospel according to Luke for nearly a year, and that Tuesday was to be our final day. We closed out the final two chapters of Luke, following which we began assembling our quarterly parish newsletter for mailing. Mind you, I'd had no food for going on forty hours. Inside, known only to me, there was a little jingle, something like this (in the tune of "ninny-nanny-boo-boo"): "I'm fasting, I'm fasting." While, on the outside (I soon found out), I was singing a different tune, something like this (think big bad lion): *Grrrrrrrrar-rchhhhhhhhhgggggggg!*

That's right, our volunteers were preparing to assemble newsletters, and in giving them some instructions, on the inside ("ninny-nanny-boo-boo")—"I'm fasting, I'm fasting," and on the outside, I was like: *Grrrrrrrrarrchhhhhhhhhgggggggg!*

I didn't even realize it until one of the fellows said, "Fr. Joseph, I'd like to give you a hug."

"Wha—" I stammered (mid-roar).

He said, "I'd like to give you a hug. In fact, I'm going to get up and come over there and give you a hug right now."

He did. It was nice. But it was so out of the ordinary, and I was kind of like, "Why?" That's when it occurred to me that I'd appeared to be roaring when inside I was (ninny-nanny) "fasting, fasting."

So I did what I had to do. I went straight downstairs to my office and ate two handfuls of party mix. As I was cramming the puffed rice mixture into my mouth, I could hardly keep my eyes open. I sat down at my desk chair and closed my eyes.

That's when someone appeared at my office door and said, "I know what you're going through, and I'd like to help."

"Who are you?" I asked.

"Who I am is not important," he said. "But I know you're fasting, and I overheard you roaring, and, as I said, I'm here to help. There's a group that meets over at the Catholic church during Lent called Lenten Fasters Anonymous. They meet tonight, seven-thirty. I'd like to take you there."

I didn't want to go. After all, I have no problem abstaining from food or restricting myself to only fasting foods. I mean, I *pride* myself on—oh well, you get the picture. It was my pride talking.

So I said, "Okay. Sure. I'll go."

"Pick you up here after Compline," he said. And he was gone.

So there I was with eight hours to worry over this unusual encounter and the one to come. The words of St. John Chrysostom came to mind:

Fasting is the change of every part of our life, because the sacrifice of the fast is not the abstinence but the distancing from sins. Therefore, whoever limits the fast to the deprivation of food, he is the one who, in reality, abhors and ridicules the fast. Are you fasting? Show me your fast with your works. Which works? If you see someone who is poor, show him mercy. If you see an enemy, reconcile with him. If you see a friend who is becoming successful, do not be jealous of him! If you see a beautiful woman on the street, pass her by.

In other words, not only should the mouth fast, but the eyes and the legs and the arms and all the other parts of the body should fast as well. Let the hands fast, remaining clean from stealing and greediness. Let the legs fast, avoiding roads which lead to sinful sights. Let the eyes fast by not fixing themselves on beautiful faces and by not observing the beauty of others. [St. John is speaking here of the sinful, passionate, objectifying gaze that distorts the beauty of another.] You are not eating meat, are you? You should not eat debauchery with your eyes as well. Let your hearing also fast. The fast of hearing is not to accept bad talk against others and sly defamations.

Let the mouth fast from disgraceful and abusive words, because what gain is there when, on the one hand, we avoid eating chicken and fish and, on the other, we chew up and consume our brothers? He who condemns and blasphemes is as if he has eaten brotherly meat, as if he has bitten into the flesh of his fellow man. It is because of this that Paul frightened us, saying: "If you chew up and consume one another, be careful that you do not annihilate yourselves."

Anyway, time flies whether you're having fun or not; so there we were, later that day, me and the stranger, heading toward my first meeting of Fasters Anonymous. On the way there, he said some of the folks at the meeting would be Roman Catholic or Episcopalian. But now that Lent had arrived for the Orthodox, the majority of the participants would be, like me, Orthodox struggling with First Week.

As we pulled into the parking lot, I understood what he meant. There were several cars with bumper stickers saying things like, "The Episcopal Church Welcomes You" and "Hate is not a family value." Then there were, "Abortion stops a beating heart," "Pray the rosary daily," and "Mary is my co-pilot."

Then I saw them, our people. There were bumper stickers spouting, "Honk 40 times if you're Orthodox," "My Church is Older than Your Church," and, of course, "Orthodoxy: Christianity, just harder."

Anyway, there were probably fifty people sitting around in a circle; I recognized a few. The meeting began with a welcome from the leader. Then, as I've already mentioned, this group sang a fasting song to the tune of the *Gilligan's Island* theme song:

> *Just stiffen that back if you're a male,*
> *Females get a grip*
> *We've started now and can't abort*
> *This forty-day trip.*

> *This plate, it's not for an ailing man,*
> *Skipping the meat de jour*
> *Six weeks it runs for Catholics*
> *For Orthodox a few days more.*

> *Fifth week it started getting rough,*
> *Many salads they were tossed,*
> *If not for the wonders of tofu*
> *The battle would be lost, the battle would be lost.*

The trip will end late one night,
As we exit that church aisle
With milk again
You can skip tofu,
Eat boiled eggs and things fried,
The Snickers bar
Mayonnaise and roast lamb,
There on Pascha bright!

As with all Twelve Step groups' open meetings, everyone was free to speak of their struggles. The first gal who spoke was obviously not Orthodox. She said, "Oh, my gosh! I swore off chocolate for Lent, and it has been, like, *so* hard." She went on and on, talking about the Galleria, Dove bars, and Starbucks.

Then this guy interrupted her and said, "Well, that's nuthin', sister, I gave up French fries! I gave up fries for Lent and I'm a truck driver! It's been hard! Hard, I tell ya!"

And so it went for about ten minutes, to the point where people were whining about potato chips, soft drinks, and candy; to the point where I was just about ready to get up and leave. Then a young man with stringy, oily, *oily* long hair began to speak. He looked so very strange I knew he must be Orthodox.

He started sobbing. He was new to Orthodoxy and he was saying how he'd misread the Scriptures and now he couldn't get all this oil out of his hair. You know that verse, Matthew 6:17, where our Lord says, "But when you fast, put oil on your head and wash your face, so it will not be obvious to men that you are fasting"? Well, this poor fellow told how he had put motor oil on his head. He did that because he knew olive oil was forbidden during the fast and Canola oil was missing from his pantry. He felt so foolish.

One by one, the tales of woe unwound: allergic reactions to shellfish; complaints of the tiny print on ingredient labels; questions about whey, Soy-Boy Not Dogs, and stuff. Then there was the man who forgot all about the fast—honestly, he said—when he consumed two Whoppers at Burger King and had a snack at Chik-fil-A.

Then there came a question from the group leader: What about almsgiving? During the fast we're encouraged to increase our giving to the poor, the less fortunate, and the beggars.

"Well, I didn't!" yelled one woman. "No sir, I passed those beggars right by, and I'd do it again if I had the chance!"

"You passed them by?" the leader asked. "Could you tell us a little more, Marge?"

"Sure. It was a middle-aged man and a teenager. They were holding signs, saying, 'Help. I'm Hungry' and 'Will work for hamburgers.'"

"Why did you pass them by? Hardness of heart, lack of cash?"

"No!" she bellowed. "Because it was my husband and my teen-aged son, that's why!"

The meeting continued with war story after war story. We consoled and encouraged one another to persevere in the fast. We ended the meeting by singing the last half of their theme song:

So this is the tale of our fasting days,
They're here for a long, long time,
We'll have to make the best of things,
It's an uphill climb.

The fasting, prayers, almsgiving too,
Will do their very best
To make us all conformable
To enjoy the Church's fest.

No bones, no wine or ice cream bars,
Avoid rotisseries,
Like red mud or Play-Doh,
Be malleable as can be.

So struggle well six weeks my friends,
You're sure to get a smile,

From seven weeks of fasting days,
Here on . . .

Bomp Bomp Bomp Bomp!

That's when there was a knock at my office door and I—*ahem*, I guess I'd been dozing. I awoke to see my boss, Fr. John, standing there singing, "Amazing grace, how sweet the sound," to the tune of *Gilligan's* theme.

Without my full wits about me, I said, "You know, I watched a lot of *Gilligan* when I was a kid, and I don't recall the castaways ever eating meat or dairy."

E.I.E.I.O.

Every Lent, letters pour into the Orthodixie headquarters, many of them dealing with what can only be said and not
written. You've all no doubt heard it—take your most accomplished
index finger, place it between your lips and make a humming sound
as you jiggle your finger up and down. Really, try it. For the sake of
spelling it out, I'll label it *e-i-e-i-o*. For instance, here's a note from
Penelope in Kentucky:

Dear Fr. Joseph,

I am new to Orthodoxy, having been received into the Church just last
year. Though English is my first, and only, language, I have learned
many foreign words and phrases since entry into the Church:

Khristos Voskrese
Xerophagy
Orthros
and . . . *Tofu.*

But this is the first year that I've ever heard the phrase [finger, lips,
humming, up and down] *e-i-e-i-o*. Is this Orthodox? What does it mean?

Also, when someone says to me *e-i-e-i-o*, how should I reply?

Penelope

Ah, yes. The fourth and fifth week of the Great Fast is the time
of year when *e-i-e-i-o* is most often heard. Penelope's letter is not the
only one; there's this:

========

Dear Fr. Joseph,

Something has gone wrong with our priest. He was always so nice and welcoming, until last night.

We got to church at 6 p.m., a half hour early, for the Presanctified Liturgy. There was a very long line for confession, but since my husband and I had prepared, we got in line. It was about 1.5 minutes before the starting time of the service when in walked Sandy Kosta with her five children, ages 2 through 6. They are very, very faithful—attending every service—much to the disappointment of most of the congregation. Let me explain: They're lovely children, but they're a little on the wild side. You see, folks light candles and put them in the stands, then the Kosta kids come along and take those lighted candles out and run around, daring any adults to chase them. It's great fun, if you're five. Like scattered bread crumbs in the forest, you can always tell when they've come to pray by the drops of wax on the floor. Our priest, God bless him, is patient and dutifully ministers to them—gently leading them in the right way.

Until, as I said, last night. Last night, he turned away from hearing my confession and, in a loud voice, shouted, *"Ek-play-so-my! Ek-play-so-my!"*

I said, "Uh, Father, that sounds like something out of *Harry Potter*." And he started weeping. After the service, though I didn't see it, folks said he was walking around the church building going like this [finger, lips, up and down]: *e-i-e-i-o.*

Carey in Quincy

========

See what I mean? It's just plain contagious this time of year in the life of the Church.

Just last week I called a priest-friend and asked, "How's it going?"

He said, "Well, everything was fine until someone dropped off a whole case of *e-i-e-i-o* at my door."

Ah, yes. All together now, to the tune of "It's Beginning to Look a Lot Like Christmas":

It's beginning to look a lot like Lent's here!
Ev'rywhere you go;
Take a look at those ladies and men frowning once again
With aches and pains and complaints galore.

It's beginning to look a lot like Lent's here!
Soy in ev'ry store
But the ugliest sight to see is the box of e-i-o-e
That will be on your own front door!

And, yes, it happens to laymen, too. Here's Chuck in Charleston:

Dear Fr. Joseph,

I need your help. My wife and I are struggling very hard to keep the whole of the Lenten Fast. But recently, there have been some problems. See, her birthday always falls during Lent and, though we keep to a pious Lenten diet, I took her out to her favorite restaurant on her big day. We discussed the menu items at length, but when the waiter arrived, my wife lost it. It went down like this: He asked if we'd like to hear the specials—we did, and my wife kept asking, "What did he say? What did he say? What did he say?"

Father, the waiter's English was perfect, though, of course, all of the specials were nowhere near fasting. I ended up ordering for my befuddled wife and it was only later, after she'd composed herself, that she explained that, no matter what the waiter mentioned in his recitation of the days' special entrees, all she'd heard was: *e-i-e-i-o*. She said that she was even afflicted with this malady when the church community sang to her on Sunday, which, she said, sounded like this:

"God grant you *e-i-e-i-o*, God grant you *e-i-e-i-o* ..."

Any advice?

Sincere Struggler

Well, yes, SS, I do have some advice, but it will be hard to bear. It goes like this: *e-i-e-i-o*! *Just* kidding. Actually, this, too, shall pass.

In his book, *The Arena*, St. Ignatius Brianchaninov writes:

> Temptations arise from the following four sources: from
> our fallen nature, from the world, from men, and from
> demons. Strictly, there is only one source of temptations:
> our fallen nature. If our nature were not in a fallen state,
> evil would never arise in us, the temptations of the world
> would have no influence on us, men would not rise up
> against one another, fallen spirits would have no occasion
> or right to approach us.

Come to think of it, that sound you make when jiggling your index
finger between humming lips is a lot like the *e-i-e-i-o* from "Old Mac-
Donald's Farm":

> *Old MacDonald tried to fast,* e-i-e-i-o!
> *And on that fast he had no chickens,* e-i-e-i-o . . .
> *No bock bock here; no bock bock there* . . .

Oh well, it doesn't really work without the "bock bock," "moo moo,"
and "oink oink," now does it? It's sort of an apophatic version of "Old
MacDonald's Farm."

But back in the old days when most folks couldn't read, *e-i-e-
i-o* was used much like we use *etc.*—or the ellipsis. (. . .) It meant:
"and so on and so forth." Thus, hymn books and service books in the
pews might say, "Our Father . . . *e-i-e-i-o*" or "I believe in One God . . .
e-i-e-i-o." Those who were illiterate knew these things by heart and
would chime in once the beginning was read. (Who knows? I might
be pulling your leg here, but bear with me.)

So, at that point in the Great Fast, when people start saying
things like *e-i-e-i-o,* it just means "and so on and so forth." Let me
explain: Having passed the midpoint of the Fast, folks are now coming down the home stretch. Some have struggled well in their prayer,
fasting, and almsgiving; others, not so much. In either case, the time
for fasting is quickly drawing to a close. And it is during these last

weeks that we are often tempted beyond what we might think necessary or bearable. Persevere! If it helps to say *e-i-e-i-o*, fine, say it.

But, just like *e-i-e-i-o*, that crazy sound (made with the finger, lips, and humming) only stands for something far greater—not just *moo-moo* or *gobble-gobble*. It could be that *e-i-e-i-o*—that is, fretting about the food, the services, the temptations, the *arrrrgggghhh!*—has become the focal point of our fasting instead of the meat, so to speak.

The "meat" of the fast is none other than our *sacrificial* offerings to God. We sacrifice time, talent, and treasure; we sacrifice our wants and desires; we sacrifice our luxury and (let's just say it)—our *fat*—to the good and merciful God in order that, unburdened by the cares of the flesh and world, we may draw closer to Him.

And if it helps, preferably when no one's near, to say *e-i-e-i-o*, go ahead! Against this, there is no law. And yet, *e-i-e-i-o* only stands for *Lord, have mercy,* or *God, be merciful to me a sinner,* or *Lord, help me!* Granted, at any time during the Fast, *e-i-e-i-o* could mean: *Oh. My. God.* But that's not really a prayer, now is it? Repeat after me: This too shall pass.

I remember one year when the children in church, mine included, had been acting up during services. They had become loud, unruly, a distraction, so much so that on a couple of Sundays I felt compelled to make announcements about the children's behavior and how the parents and adults needed to help out. *Please!*

Soon afterward I went down to a monastery for a few days of retreat and made my confession. A week or so after I returned, a parishioner came up to me and, with a smile on her face, said, "Father, I've noticed that the children have been acting better in church since you went to confession."

Heh!

And there it is: confession. Confession just may be what the doctor ordered to help cure the malady of *e-i-e-i-o*. Struggle well, in the final weeks of the Fast. For it won't be long before, well, *e-i-e-i-o*.

Two Miles till Pascha

Back in high school, my football coach required all the players who were not also on the baseball team to run track in the off season. (Then there was that one year that we had a competing volleyball team, but it was a different time, and I won't tell you what the ol' coach thought of boys playin' volleyball.) Of course, his goal was to keep us in good shape. So springtime was track time.

Now, look at me. Do I look like a track star to you? For those of you unable to see me at the moment, let me just say, the answer to that question is, "Uh, no."

But there I was for our first track meet, my first one ever, and if memory serves, I believe I was signed up to put the shot, fling the discus, and maybe run the first leg of a relay race. No biggie; typical lineman fare.

Then the coach came in before the meet to give us a pep talk and to inform us that the little fellow who was signed up to run the two-mile was sick. We needed a replacement.

No one raised their hand to volunteer. Y'all, *pfff*, two miles? Hello! *Two* miles! Come on! I could do that, I reasoned. So without further hesitation, I raised my hand. I volunteered.

My coach, a much smarter man than I, looked at me like I had six heads. The other track team members looked at me with what I thought was awe and admiration. A faint smile came upon the coach's lips and he asked, "Are you sure? Two miles is eight laps around the track, Huneycutt."

Pfff. Get out! I used to run two miles near my house all the time.

It was one mile from my house up to the crossroads in the little town called Palestine. I used to run that regularly to keep in shape. Besides, that route even included hills! So what if there were eight laps—at least they would be flat!

"Sure I'm sure," I said.

"Okay," he said.

Actually, if I remember correctly, he asked me about five times if I was sure I wanted to do this. And, as you've no doubt already gathered, each time I said, "Yes."

So there I was, lined up against three other guys. They looked skinny and long compared to me. *Hunh*, no problem; I'd jogged for two miles on many, many occasions, boys. Don't get your hopes up!

The gun sounded and off from our starting positions we ran. Y'all, would you believe I was out in front from the start? *Mmm-hmm.*

As I was rounding the first turn I looked back and, *heh heh*, those poor ol' skinny boys were long behind me. Oh sure, I remembered the coach telling me that I was going to have to pace myself; it was a long run, etc. But as we completed the first of eight laps, me with my homies in the stands cheering me on, I was starting to come to the conclusion that I was, that's right, superhuman. Without a doubt, I thought, I might just be invincible.

As we rounded the corner and began the second lap, I started to hear some panting behind me. Yep, one of those guys was gaining. "Bring it on," I thought! Bring. It. On.

Well, he did.

As we began the third of eight laps, this fellow was right there beside me. I'd given up thoughts of grandeur and had convinced myself that second place, especially on such short notice, would not be a bad finish at all.

By the fourth or fifth lap, I was no longer first, nor second, but I was third out of four runners. And there was no way I was gonna let that loser behind me pass me. No sirree.

Okay. You've no doubt already passed me in storytelling, and you're right. I lost. Not only that, but I ended up running almost the entire last lap solo.

My homies in the stands were no longer paying me any attention. Marvel Comics had withdrawn their contract for the new superhero, Flash Huneycutt, and, quite frankly, by run's end, I was happy—beyond grateful—that the race was over and I was still breathing.

Whew.

Which brings me to the business of the Great Fast of Lent: The Church in her wisdom has provided us with an easy start. Unlike the firing of the pistol at a track meet, we have the fast-free week following the Sunday of the Publican & Pharisee, the regular week after Prodigal Son Sunday, a week without meat—Cheesefare—which is otherwise fast-free, and finally, the first week of the Great Fast.

Many people keep this week very strictly. Frankly, that works well for me. Then comes that second lap—or week—of the fast, the third, and fourth, and so on. Somewhere along the line, it may seem as if the progress you're making is just not adding up, or that something big and bad—whatever it is—is coming up behind you to overtake you.

Well, first, let's take the adding up part. Like that famous equation where someone asks, "Would you rather I give you one million dollars today, or give you a penny and double that amount each day for thirty days?" What would you say?

Of course, those who answer one million dollars today are quite content in their good fortune. But they will have shortchanged themselves. For the person who answered, "I'll take one penny to be doubled each day for thirty days," will have only one cent today, two cents tomorrow, and four cents after three days. So far, not so good.

After a week, he will have 64 cents. After 15 days—$163.84. And after three whole weeks—only $10,485.76.

Now, by this point, just like yours truly competing in that two-mile race, the person with the million dollars in his pocket seems the obvious winner. (After all, I led that race for about four laps.) But, in reality, at the end of the thirty days, the person who chose the penny-a-day-doubled-each-day-for-a-month ends up with $5,368,709.12!

You may say, "Okay, fine. What does this have to do with the Great Fast of Lent?"

The answer: "Everything."

First of all, we have to run the race. Secondly, we struggle to win. Win? Yes, we struggle to win our salvation through our ascetical exercises, which temper the flesh. But, most importantly, we struggle to build up treasure in heaven. That's right—the winning is not this side of Paradise. But the battle is. The race is on!

What about us? Well, we're given a penny—a talent, if you will—that is doubled, multiplied even greater than double, by the Giver of all good things, the Good God and Father of all.

How is this penny doubled? It is multiplied by the good that we do. What happens when we miss a day? When we skip those good deeds—that prayer, that fasting, that almsgiving?

What happens when that runner falls? Or that wide receiver is tackled? Is the game over? Do all the fans in the stands just say, "Oh, well, he fell down. It's time to go home." No! The fans, like the saints who've gone before, continue to cheer us on!

We fall down . . .
We get back up . . .
We fall down . . .
We get back up . . .

And we continue to run the race, with the loving support of that "great cloud of witnesses," who all affirm that the goal is indeed worth running the race with endurance.

> Therefore we also, since we are surrounded by so great a
> cloud of witnesses, let us lay aside every weight, and the sin
> which so easily ensnares us, and let us run with endurance
> the race that is set before us, looking unto Jesus, the author

and finisher of our faith, who for the joy that was set before Him endured the cross, despising the shame, and has sat down at the right hand of the throne of God. For consider Him who endured such hostility from sinners against Himself, lest you become weary and discouraged in your souls. (Hebrews 12:1–3)

These witnesses, the saints who've run the race before us, speak to us through the ages by their deeds, those "pennies" multiplied by faith and stored in the treasury of heaven for those who persevere in faith.

Question: So what of the Fast?
Answer: *Do better than you did last year.*

What's that you say? You fasted perfectly from food? Then struggle to pray more fervently. You say you pray night and day? Then give alms to the poor sacrificially. And if there's anything we learn from even the most worthy examples of faith, it's that no matter what ascetical feat one endures, the perfection is always found *only in Christ*—for all have fallen short of the glory.

Like that famous equation that yields a much greater reward for the penny that is doubled daily, we must beware of the quick fix offered by the riches of this world and, by our good deeds, multiply that heavenly treasure. This is the reason for the race.

And, if you'll forgive me, I'll mention one of my pet peeves which one often hears this time of year: "Do the best you can."

Do the best you can?

Now brothers and sisters, that's a recipe for failure; heck, sinner that I am, the best I can do is what has got me to where I am! We don't give an inexperienced bunch of players a ball, with no practice whatsoever, and say, "Okay, it's game time. Do the best you can."

No! We practice and practice and practice; we fall down, get back up—struggling to do better. We will never reach perfection if we just do the best *we* can. Rather, as always, we are perfected in Christ. He is perfection. All our efforts, unworthy though they be, are perfected by grace in Christ.

This is the reason for our prayer—*perfection in Christ.*

This is the reason for our almsgiving—*perfection in Christ.*

This is the reason for our fasting—*perfection in Christ.*

It is not about *us* doing the best that *we* can. Rather, the race of faith is run by swift and strong, slow and weak alike, toward perfection in Christ. For if our prayer, almsgiving, and fasting are not toward our perfection in Christ, then they're all in vain. Like any journey, this one begins with one step—one step, followed by the next step.

Those efforts, cheered on by the saints, are multiplied beyond measure by the Giver of all good things, in the treasury of heaven. For, as the Orthros aposticha from Tuesday of Cheese Week says:

> If thou dost fast from food, my soul, yet dost not cleanse thyself from passions, thou dost rejoice in vain over thine abstinence. For if thy purpose is not turned towards amendment of life, as a liar thou art hateful in God's sight, and thou dost resemble the evil demons who never eat at all. Do not by sinning make the fast worthless, but firmly resist all wicked impulses. Picture to thyself that thou art standing beside the crucified Savior or rather, that thou art thyself crucified with Him who was crucified for thee; and cry out to Him: Remember me, O Lord, when Thou comest in Thy Kingdom.

As we come to the Great Fast, together as the Bride of Christ, the Church, let us love one another and bear each other's burdens. For our Lord says, "If anyone desires to come after Me, let him deny himself, and take up his cross, and follow Me" (Matthew 16:24). "He who endures to the end shall be saved" (Mark 13:13).

The best we can? That's not good enough. But, *the best we can is* multiplied mightily by the wood of the cross. When we fall down, we climb back up by way of the cross.

> And if anyone sins, we have an Advocate with the Father, Jesus Christ the righteous. And He Himself is the propitiation for our sins, and not for ours only but also for the whole world. (1 John 2:1–2)

Let us enter the fast as if it were our last, so that in dying to the passions, we may be alive to God in Christ and rise with Him at His glorious Pascha, in the very hope of the Resurrection which is to come.

Baby Jesus by the Chimney

Did you read about that Baby Jesus that was recently stolen from someone's yard? Oh, I'm sure more than one Baby Jesus has been stolen this year, perhaps even in your town! I decided to do something about it. I became an investigator. The other day I went door to door in my neighborhood in search of Baby Jesus.

My first stop was the home of Minerva Simmons, aged 73, on Tomball Drive. She's the owner of the giant crèche scene. You know, with the big plastic light-up Mary and Joseph, wise men, manger, and the optional star on a pole?

As I pulled into her driveway, it was crystal clear that something was missing. The manger was empty; it was just a cradle for hay. Yep, Baby Jesus was MFM: missing from manger. In the place where the plastic body normally lay was a sign that read, "Have you seen me?" with a picture of Baby Jesus. (Well, you know what I mean.)

Friends, I'll spare you further details, but Mrs. Simmons was devastated. This plastic Baby Jesus had been in her family since the 1970s, when her kids were young. It meant the world to her.

Silly me, I don't know why, but I asked her if it had been made in China. She said, "No, Malaysia." Malaysia is, of course, predominantly Muslim, and I briefly contemplated them making a plastic baby named "Jesus" as opposed to a stuffed Teddy bear named "Mohammed"—oh, never mind.

But that wasn't the strangest part of my day. After getting a good description of the missing plastic Jesus, I moseyed on over to Home Depot to pick up some sleuthing tools. I could hardly get around in the parking lot thanks to all the Christmas trees. Then I noticed that all of these trees were not only wet, they were each topped with a tiny cross! "Well, that's interesting," I thought.

Then I saw something weird: There was a big above-ground swimming pool in the midst of the trees, and—oh my goodness—who could stand it? There was a preacher bellowing his message over the loudspeaker: "Repent! Repent! Repent!"

I stopped the car, got out, and asked a tree worker, "What's going on?"

He said, "Preacher John's here to put Christ back into Christmas!"

I looked up to the pool platform and there stood Preacher John, in a robe, soaking wet. I said, "Y'all are baptizing out here in the parking lot full of trees at Home Depot?"

"Yep! Ain't it great? Forty-eight so far today!" the preacher yelled.

"Souls?" I asked.

"No! Trees! These here beauties were once only holiday trees; now, having been baptized, they are Christmas trees!"

I was befuddled. "You are kidding, right?"

"Son," the preacher said, "what brought you here today?"

"Actually, I'm looking for the Baby Jesus." (Y'all, I knew I shouldn't have said it as soon as I did!)

He yelled, "Hallelujah!" Which I interpreted as "last call for nutball." I jumped in my car and sped away (sans tools) to my next destination. It was the home of Earl Goins.

Earl was, apparently, very patriotic. His home was decorated in red, white, and blue; I mean *only* red, white, and blue. There were patriotic Christmas lights, red, white, and blue wreaths, and little American flags, hundreds of them, all over his yard.

I said, "What's with the flags & colors?"

He said, "Boy, are you an American?"

I said, "Well, yeah—"

He said, "Well, then, you ought to know it's Christmas!"

I said, "Yes, sir, but—"

He yelled, "But nuthin'! Look over across the street. See that house, the way it's decorated? It's gonna be the ruination of this great land, I tell you—Mexicans, Mexicans, Mexicans."

I looked across the street, then back at Earl, and said, "But, sir, that's the home of the Venderswits. They're from Norway."

"Oh," he said, "okay, but what about the house next to them? It's also all decked in red and green. Last name: Lopez."

"Right . . . uh, they've been in the United States for fifty-three years, sir," I said.

"Well, that may be, but this red and green, red and green is gettin' O.L.D. Whatever happened to the ol' red, white, and blue?"

You know, I should have known better, but foolishly I said, "Mr. Goins, red and green may be the colors of Mexico's flag, but they're also the traditional colors for Christmas."

And immediately he said, "What are you, boy, some sort of pagan?"

Needless to say, I didn't think Mr. Earl Goins knew where the Baby Jesus was. So I quickly said the Pledge of Allegiance with him—shouting the words "under God"—and hastened on my way.

As I rode down the street, I witnessed a very heated argument on the sidewalk between two middle-aged women. One was shouting "Happy Holidays!" The other was yelling "Merry Christmas!" These ladies were very upset, red in the face, and almost to the point of blows. Then they spotted me cruising by, staring at them. They both yelled at me something I can't repeat here (but it means the same as *Bah Humbug*!).

This searching for the Baby Jesus thing was turning out to be more than I'd bargained for. I decided to take a break. I popped into a Starbuck's for a much-needed Soy Mocha Latte Grande Triple. I was sitting there minding my own business, staring at my Franklin-Covey planner like I was planning something, when up walked a total stranger who handed me three tracts.

One was about how the candy cane was made in the shape of a

"J" for Jesus and the red stripes represent His blood. Another tract told how the song "The Twelve Days of Christmas" was actually an instructional song about Catholicism, with hidden meanings to prevent persecution: two turtledoves = the Old and New Testaments; nine ladies dancing = the nine gifts of the Holy Spirit; twelve drummers drumming = the twelve points of doctrine in the Creed, etc. Oh, and the Partridge in the Pear Tree? Well, that's Jesus! (Incidentally, neither of these legends is true.)

The third gift was a printout of a popular email that purports to be a letter from none other than *Jesus* about Christmas! I don't read many of those mass email forwards, but this letter from Jesus concerning Christmas made some good points, one of which was this (mind you, this is "our Lord" speaking): "Finally, if you want to make a statement about your belief in and loyalty to Me, then behave like a Christian. Let people know by your actions that you are one of Mine."

I thought about that one for a moment. It drove home the point that enforcing our own petty views, slogans, decorations, and rituals on others as a means of proving our Christianity—how very Christian we are—is just plain wrong.

It reminded me of the fellow—well, this is how my trek finally ended. There was a house I passed where I noticed a plastic Santa Claus lying in the manger. I stopped, got out of my car, and was on my way up to the house when I noticed the roof. Up on the roof, in front of a few plastic reindeer, was—you're not going to believe this: a plastic Baby Jesus—on the roof!

I thought I'd found the prize! I was curious, however, as to why Baby Jesus was up on the roof by the chimney. I rang the bell. A twelve-year-old boy answered the door and asked, "What's the password?"

I said, "I'm looking for the Baby Jesus."

"Well! Come on in!" he yelled as he flung open the door.

I said, "No, I, uh—wait! That was the password?"

"Yep," he said. "Didn't you notice He was up on the roof?"

"I did," I said, "but I have no idea why. Tell me, is that Jesus from Malaysia?" At that, he slammed the door. I was dumbfounded.

A neighbor saw me standing there and came up to me. She explained, "That's the home of the Sawyers. They're new to Christianity. They were always so very much into Santa, never paying any mind to Christ—that is, until they were baptized earlier this week over in the Home Depot parking lot while buying their tree. They made a promise that from now on, Santa and Jesus would swap places; it would be only Jesus who came down their chimney!"

Speaking of goofy, that's when the policeman pulled up by the curb and asked what was going on. (The little boy had apparently called them and told them about me.) I told the officer that I was in search of the Baby Jesus who'd been stolen, it was in the paper and all—and, with him observing me, would he mind if I climbed up on that roof to see if that Baby Jesus had been made in Malaysia.

He thought I was a total kook but, amazingly, he let me do it. So with the help of the neighbor's ladder, I climbed, ever so carefully, up the steep roof of the house. I've never been a fan of heights, and just past the gutters I was wishing that, rather than me having to climb up, ol' Jesus would just come down!

My foot slipped. I panicked and gasped, "God help me!" Regaining my footing, I made my way quickly up to the top of the roof, and there I had an epiphany. I could see all around the neighborhood. It was amazing. As dusk was setting in, I could see that virtually all the homes were decorated with lights and trees and candles, with wisps of smoke rising from their chimneys. There were kids playing in the yards, and you could tell, everyone was expectant. There were moms pulling packages from their trunks, dads hiding stuff in the garage, and smells of desserts being baked in a half-dozen kitchens. What was the reason for all this commotion, all this festivity, all this expecting?

You guessed it. I looked down at the Baby Jesus by the chimney, and I realized that He *did* come down! No matter how much we moan and gripe and cry about this and that not being the right way—whether to do the Santa thing, the St. Nicholas thing, both or neither—I mean, you can wish and want *all* you want but, thank God, you just can't stop it: Christmas.

I looked back down at the blonde-haired, blue-eyed Baby (good grief, talk about goofy) and turned it over, hoping it was not the stolen one made in Malaysia. I actually breathed a sigh of relief when I read the words, "Made in China."

China. Wow. Now there's a thought! You want to make a difference? You want to preach the real meaning of God coming down, taking human flesh in the Virgin, proclaiming the good news of salvation, dying to destroy death and all that? There's only one other place I can think of that needs that healing news more than China! And that, brothers and sisters, is our own heart; for if you can't find the Baby Jesus there, you won't be able to find Him anywhere.

I thanked the cop and the neighbor, got back in my car, and as it was growing dark, I headed toward home. That's when I spotted him: a little boy with a red wagon walking down the street. And in the wagon was the figure of the Baby Jesus.

So I pulled up to the boy and said, "Son, where did you get that little Baby Jesus that's in your wagon?"

The boy replied, "I got him from Mrs. Simmons' yard."

"And why did you take him?" I asked.

The little boy replied, "Well, last year, I prayed to the Lord Jesus. I told Him if He would bring me a red wagon for Christmas, I would give Him a ride around the block in it. I'm just now getting around to it. You gotta be faithful, Mister, if you want Him to stick with ya!"

"Wait," I said, "you don't actually believe that the Lord Jesus comes down your chimney on Christmas Eve, do ya?"

"What, are you crazy?" cried the little boy. "I ain't never heard that one before. But I do know that all good things come down from God, and sometimes He even uses my folks to teach me about anonymous giving. I go along with it. It's all good. People get a little kooky this time of year, though—even Christians.

"Anyway, if you'll excuse me now, I gotta get this here Baby back to Mrs. Simmons before that cop comes back 'round again."

And with that, he was gone, and my mission was ended. Well, almost. I realized, even more so, the work I had yet to do on my own heart. The heart: *that's* where you'll find the Lord. Search for Him— there.

The Ghost of Past Christmas Presents

It had to be either holiday stress, or my habit of eating garlic in the evening—or a combination of both—but one December I had a couple of dreams involving ghosts similar to those found in Charles Dickens' *A Christmas Carol*. I was visited by one specter regarding the past and a second concerning the future. Thus, the third one seemed inevitable.

There I was all tucked in bed the Monday night before Christmas reading *The Island of the Day Before,* by Umberto Eco, when I could no longer keep my eyes open. There are side benefits to reading Eco. As with reading Vladimir Lossky's *Mystical Theology of the Eastern Church*, you are *guaranteed* to get to sleep! Don't get me wrong, Lossky's classic is one of my favorite books, but, as I tell everyone, you end up reading it three times before you finish it the first time, because each night you forget you already read that page the night before, just before you fell asleep.

Anyway, it was 9:30 Central time when I fell asleep, only to be awakened by a shrill cry. Oh my! I roused myself from my bed of slumber only to see that lights were still on in the house. I also noted, staggering toward the bedroom door, that it was only 10:30.

I hastened down the hall and around the corner to see my wife and oldest daughter glued to the satellite feed on the computer screen, cheering on the Carolina Panthers (who were on their way to whipping the Tampa Bay Buccaneers).

"Sorry, Dad!"

Arrgh . . .

On the way back to bed, trying to get a jump on returning to sleep by not fully opening my eyes, out of the corner of my eye I spotted the lighted Christmas tree. I also saw our black cat, Lily. Those, dear readers, were my final waking memories as I hit the pillow and fell into a deep, deep sleep: A cat, a Christmas tree . . . a cat . . . a Christmas tree . . . cat . . . mas . . . a ca . . . a Kawa . . . a k-k-w-w-ass www kiss wa—*a Kawasaki?*

Rimmm-nnn—Rimmmn-n-n-n-n—Rimmm-nnnnnnn! He was flying down our hallway, some guy on a Kawasaki motorcycle.

Wha—? And there he was beside me, astride his two-wheeled ride.

I stammered, "Are you the Ghost of Christmas Present?"

"Nope, I'm the Ghost of Past Christmas Presents!" the fellow replied.

"But I never got a motorcycle," I said. "You must have the wrong guy."

He checked his list. "Did you get:

"Banana seat Schwinn with green metallic paint?"

"Yep."

"Elephant leg bell bottoms?"

"Absolutely."

"Purple velvet platform shoes?"

"Well, yeah."

"Trampoline?"

"Unh-huh."

"Truckloads of 45s and record albums?"

"Heh! You got it!"

"Mood ring?"

"Hmmm." *(sigh)*

"Several GI Joes?"

"I ain't ashamed."

"Four stereos, six sets of speakers, electric guitar, drum set?"

"That would be me."

"Patient parents?"

"Aha! I told you you had the wrong guy!"

"Believe me son, with a list like this, they were!" he said. "Oh! Wait a minute . . . Baltimore Colts football jacket? The *Baltimore Colts*?"

"Look," I explained, "it was on sale that year at K-Mart; my mom didn't know any better."

"This can't be right: Buzz Lightyear? I must have the wrong guy."

"No," I said, "that's me. I like Buzz Lightyear."

"But when *was* that?" he asked.

"I dunno, six, seven years ago," I said. "That's what I wanted, a talking Buzz Lightyear. My wife gave it to me."

"I see," he said. "So you pretty much always get what you want for Christmas?"

"Wait a minute," I exclaimed. "Who are you? Look, I've read Dickens' *A Christmas Carol*, I've seen movie versions and cartoon versions; you're supposed to be the Ghost of Christmas Present. This is where you show me the streets of London—or Charlotte, or Houston—on the current Christmas morning. We're supposed to observe the meager but happy Christmas celebrations of the Cratchit family, or some such, and the sweet nature of their lame son Tiny Tim, with some ominous foreboding of pending tragedy thrown in. Then I'm supposed to see what people really think of me, and somewhere along the line I, a cold-hearted old man, am supposed to have a change of heart, sort of like the Grinch . . ."

"No," he replied, "I am not the Ghost of Christmas Present. I am the Ghost of Past Christmas Presents; different story."

I was confused. "Okay, so what's next?"

Rimmm-nnn—Rimmmn-n-n-n-n—Rimmm-nnnnnnn! He revved the Kawasaki's engine and said, "Hop on!"

Y'all, I didn't wanna. It was a small motorcycle and I'm a big ol' boy. But, as dreams go, there we were flying down the road, the wind whipping through my thinning hair, speeding around curves, flying through yellow lights, going off road, and jumping through the air like E.T. on his pedal bike . . . and that's when—

CRASH!

As I lay on the pavement, which felt a whole lot like my bed, I opened my eyes. They fluttered in the darkness. You know how it works: It was my bed, but it was the pavement, there was my wife and my cat, but there was also just me and the motorcycle. (I had no idea where the Ghost of Evel Kneivel, or whoever he was, had gone.) All I knew was, back in full-dream mode, I could hear a siren in the distance.

And it suddenly occurred to me: The motorcycle was a 1976 Kawasaki KE 125. As they were bundling me up and hoisting me into the ambulance, the back story on the bike flashed vividly before me. I was fifteen years old and my high school was raffling off a 1976 Kawasaki KE 125 motorcycle. Though we were Baptists, and gambling ranked high on God's big list of no-nos, after much begging my mom bought me a ticket, *one* ticket, for that motorcycle.

I was absolutely convinced—beyond a doubt, positive—that I, ladies and gentlemen, had *the* winning ticket! I was going to win that bike. It was displayed at every Varsity basketball game in the school's hallway. It was blue, my favorite color, and somewhere on it was the number 8, which was my favorite number.

I hope you'll forgive me this silliness, but that bike and I shared a bond. It was love, love at first sight; and, by goodness, come the drawing, just in time for Christmas, it was going to be mine.

All mine, I say!

MINE!

"Who are you talking to?"

Wha—?

It sounded like my wife's voice, but all I could see was the Ghost of Past Christmas Presents, surrounded by a host of doctors and nurses. I was in the hospital. And that's where this dream got really weird. (Which does bring up the question: Are there any normal dreams?)

What happened next was: I floated up out of my body, like a spirit myself, and was joined, hovering above my body and the hospital staff, by my guide, the Ghost of Past Christmas Presents.

We traveled down a long hallway and entered a room full of tons of stuff. I said, "What is all this?"

"It's all the things you received as gifts throughout all of your Christmases," the ghost replied.

Some of it I recalled, but many of the things I'd totally forgotten. But the room was too loud, much too noisy, and in my slumber I stirred. I really wanted to wake up . . . so much stuff . . . it was . . .

Then the door slammed and we entered another room. In this room, there was nothing but people: joyful people, singing!

There were folks in the mountains of North Carolina singing Christmas carols, all dressed in festive array and freezing as they sang, only to be invited into warm and happy homes for a gladsome repast.

There was my mom, the prettiest one in the bunch, singing with the choir for our Baptist Church cantata.

There were Orthodox Christians, having just celebrated the Nativity Liturgy, kneeling in church with candles and singing old favorites and festal songs before the icon of the Theotokos, Virgin and Child.

There was the old Arab lady who'd vowed that if her son was healed of cancer she would sing the Christmas Kontakion solo in church:

Today the Virgin gives birth to the incomprehensible One,
and the earth offers a cave to the unapproachable One;
Angels and shepherds glorify Him;
the wise men journey with a star;
since for our sakes is born the Eternal God, as a little Child.

Then there was one of my favorites, Handel's *Messiah*, with the Hallelujah Chorus being sung by a group of high school students.

At that point, I totally forgot whatever ailed me. Handel'll do that to you.

Blaise Pascal wrote, "We seek happiness in illusory diversions, hoping to forget our mortality." That night, in that dream, with all of those dear folks singing the praises of the Incarnate God, I forgot my mortality. Yet, with all weighty respect to the choirs, carolers, Christmas Kontakion and Handel to boot, the credit should actually be laid at the feet of virtue. It is rare, this side of paradise, for us to seek that forgetting of mortality in virtue. We most certainly seek it in vice—in our greed, materialism, consumerism, and selfish desires.

As one priest said, "We sin because we die." Think about it; isn't it because we know the eventuality, but don't know the time, that we rush forward to cram so much into so little? And what does it leave us but full of remorse and empty of charity?

On the other hand, there are times when, planned or otherwise, the hoping to forget mortality is wrapped in beauty and appears as a sacrifice pleasing to the Good God. That must be what Handel meant when, upon completion of *Messiah*, he said, "I did see all heaven open before me and the great God Himself."

Hallelujah!

Sing, "Hallelujah!"

"Beeeeeeeeeeeeeeeeeeeeeeeeeeeeeee," rang out the heart monitor.

"Uh oh," I gasped. "What happened? Did I die?"

"No," said the Ghost of Past Christmas Presents. "Look."

We were back in the hospital room, hovering over the bed, and there, sadly (well, kinda), lay a lifeless motorcycle, consigned to the dustbin of things that might have been but, thank God, weren't. And still, the voices of the chanters, singers, and trumpets rang in my ears.

Then the hospital bed shrank and became filled with straw; the hospital personnel took on the garb of the shepherds and wise men, and there appeared a host of heavenly angels filling the room.

"Stop it," said my guide. "Stop right there, son. You're fashioning your own dream."

"Why?" I asked. "This is the good part, the best part, the coming of God in the flesh!"

"Not yet," he said. "You're not ready yet; there's more to be done. Besides, that's not my place."

"Oh no," I cried. "Please don't tell me I have to wait for the Ghost of Christmas Future!"

"No," he said, "your dreams have ended. But prepare yourself—not so much with gifts, and cards, and trinkets and tomtinkers and bazookers."

"Kawasakis?" I whispered.

"Right, no Kawasakis," he said. "But prepare yourself for worship; prepare your children for worship. It's not so much, as the popular saying goes, that we should keep Christ in Christmas, but we should prepare ourselves to keep the Mass in Christmas. For it is our worship of God Incarnate that will reign forever, even after all these material things—even the earth itself—have passed away.

"For the day draws nigh," continued my guide. "The Savior, Christ the Lord, is come to save the world. Let us prepare minds, hearts, and souls to sing the praises like the pilgrims, even the shepherds before us who said, 'Let us go over to Bethlehem and see this thing that has happened, which the Lord has made known to us'—and who returned, glorifying and praising God for all they had heard and seen, as it had been told them."

As I awoke from this nocturnal visitation, even in my groggy state, I understood that there is no greater present to be given than that which was in the past, is now, and shall be forever—which is Christ the Lord.

Part III

You Preach Most What You Most Need to Learn

Bending the Rules
Out of Love

Have you ever known a staunch rule-follower? I mean someone who seems obsessed, good and bad, with following rules?

Me? Hey, I'm a lists person. I like to check things off: did this, doing that, need to do that. Back when I did my clinical training at a state mental hospital, my fellow chaplains joked that when I died, I'd check that (life) off the list, too! And, if you promise not to pick on me, I'll admit I'm pretty big on the rule-following thing.

I'm fairly certain that if something tragic happened and everyone on the planet was suddenly vaporized except for me, I'd probably still stop at red lights until they turned green. Then again, if you've ever driven in Houston, you know it's true: I'd better hope I was the only one stopping at the red light, because if there was only one other driver in Houston—he'd surely rear-end me right then and there! Then, of course, I'd want to swap insurance info, even though, being the only two people left on the planet and all—oh, well, you get the picture.

Then there's love. Love messes with the rules. Love changes the rules. But before I get to the love stuff, let's start with something I know more about: football. That's right, football. I probably know more about football than I do about love, and as they say, "You preach most what you most need to learn." So bear with me.

I'll start with my high school football coach. Not that he was tall, muscular, or imposing, mind you; but Coach Jim Cullivan was a giant. He was a rough and country ol' hillbilly, but he was also a psychological master. He got in your head. It began with the gimlet eye. Coach Cullivan had piercing eyes that, whether he was aware of it or not, saw into your secret chest, where you hid yourself. If he liked what he saw, he brought it out and made you keep it. If he didn't, he helped you to maim, pillage, and kill it.

As with most giants in my life, I hated him. That's the way the dance begins. Akin to break-dancing, the initial dance with giants is rough, awkward, and painful. Then there's the slow dance that's comforting and understandable. And when the dance is almost over, though you don't know it until it is, the party really begins. It ends too soon. But you know how to dance—all by yourself.

"The frost is on the pumpkin!" was Coach Cullivan's seasonal mantra. What he meant was that the games were about to begin. After four to six weeks of practice, even the weather was getting ready to participate in the sport of the gods: football.

What does this have to do with love, you might ask? Patience; I'll get to that in a minute. For now, bookmark the football stuff and travel back with me to my childhood.

Back when I was a kid, I really wanted a certain rock album for Christmas. I'm pretty sure my parents did not want the album in their house. In other words, the answer was "No." Imagine my surprise when on Christmas Eve, while unwrapping presents with our extended family, I ripped away the pretty paper to reveal the outrageous cover of the new KISS album! Now I'd say it's a pretty safe bet that my grandmother didn't like the looks of the album's cover, and an even safer bet that, though more than thirty years have passed, she's never heard a single KISS song. But, hey, she knew I wanted it, she loved me, and, well, that was the rule: love.

Then there was the time on the church softball field when a chubby catcher (that would be me) was assisting in trying to walk a big ol' country boy to first base. He was a homerun threat, and I was dutifully stepping wide of home plate to walk him when he leaned way over and swung, narrowly missing my head. I could hear my mom yelling at him from the stands. Then, on the next pitch, he stepped out of the batter's box and hit, not only the ball, but my glove with it. The ball, and my glove, went sailing. A loud moan rose from the stands, but greater than that was the look on that big ol' boy's face as my mother met him at second base! Sure, a mom on the playing field was against the rules. But there was no doubt she loved me!

Okay, change the channel back to football. In the off season, all football players were required to take fifth-period gym class with Coach Cullivan. Actually, it wasn't just in the off season; during season we simply began practice early. Anyway, Coach would have us do some silly things to improve our coordination. One such activity was playing basketball, full court, with a football. And yes, we had to (try to) dribble.

In addition to calisthenics, running, and weight lifting, we also had to wrestle each other. Coach would normally pair opponents who were fairly equal in strength and agility. Competition helped to build character, and what good was a character puffed up by weaker opponents?

Some guys, however, just never get with the program. Not everyone is thrilled to work up a sweat. Joe Ross was one of those who weren't. During times of random rotation, everyone on the team enjoyed wrestling Joe. He was an easy pin. You could tell he had a complex of some sort. He didn't want to be there. God bless him, he looked like a loser.

One day, after he'd lost his third consecutive match, Coach Cullivan yanked him up off the mat and slapped him across the face. Ross flinched, his fists balled. Cullivan yelled, "Hit me!"

Ross, who was tearing up, said, "I can't hit you, Coach."

Cullivan hauled off and slapped him again. Stunned, red-faced, and crying, Ross again flinched. He almost brought up a hand. Through tears he said, "I can't hit you, Coach."

Somewhere during the pregnant pause, Ross decided to pat the Coach across the cheek.

"Dammit, Ross, I said, 'hit me!'" With that Coach Cullivan went to hit the boy again and Joe Ross slapped the fool out of Jim Cullivan. "Now get down there and wrestle," Coach Cullivan said.

Joe Ross beat every single boy on the team that afternoon. Though we were all amazed, no one was more surprised than Mr. Ross. I've not seen him since graduation, but I've got to believe his life changed that day—the day Coach Cullivan bent the rules out of love.

Of your charity, please bear with one more adolescent tale. You know how boys like to show off. Well, it was the summer, I was eleven or twelve, and some of us kids were taking turns hot-doggin' it, jumping off the pier into the lake, trying to outdo each other.

That's when I had the bright idea of turning a flip in the air between the wooden ladder rails. I still remember it like it was yesterday: my right leg leaving the grasp of my hands and banging against the old wooden slats. Then, there was that big pool of blood. As I got out of the water, especially to my adolescent eyes it looked like you could see past the bone, clear down to China, in my knee.

That's when my dad took over. He got me into the old Chevrolet Impala and sped the 20-mile trek to the hospital. Although I was holding the towel that was turning red with my own blood, I was concerned when I looked over to see that my dad was driving over 100 miles per hour. Y'all, I'm a rule-follower from way back, and I said, "Dad, slow down! I don't want you to get a speeding ticket." He said, "Don't worry, I won't. Besides, if a cop comes, he can lead us to the hospital."

He didn't get a ticket. I got twelve stitches. And, although he broke the rules, there was no doubt he loved me.

I hope you've got your own family stories, where it suddenly occurred to you that there's a difference in breaking the rules—and bending the rules out of love.

And when He came near the gate of the city, behold, a dead man was being carried out, the only son of his mother; and she was a widow. And a large crowd from the city was with her. When the Lord saw her, He had compassion on her and said to her, "Do not weep." Then He came and touched the open coffin, and those who carried him stood still. And He said, "Young man, I say to you, arise." So he who was dead sat up and began to speak. And He presented him to his mother.

Then fear came upon all, and they glorified God, saying, "A great prophet has risen up among us"; and, "God has visited His people." And this report about Him went throughout all Judea and all the surrounding region. (Luke 7:12–17)

So, you see, even God—especially God—does the same: time and again He bends the rules out of love.

He bent the rules out of love when an old couple named Joachim and Anna were blessed with a child—even a girl.

He bent the rules out of love when He emptied Himself and took on the form of a servant—bearing our skin, the skin of mortality.

He bent the rules out of love when Joachim & Anna's daughter, a virgin, conceived and bore a child, the Son of God.

That same Son bent the rules out of love—healing on the Sabbath.

He bent the rules out of love by saying to those who (following the law) wished to stone the woman caught in adultery, "Those without sin cast the first stone."

He bent the rules out of love when He conversed with the woman at the well.

He bent the rules out of love when He multiplied the loaves and fishes.

He bent the rules out of love when He walked on water to calm the fears of His disciples.

He bent the rules out of love when He called forth Lazarus, four days dead, from the tomb.

And although He told Mary Magdalene not to touch Him

(because He'd yet to ascend to His Father), He bent the rules out of love when He said to Thomas, "Put out your hand."

He bent the rules out of love when He unconfused the tongues of simple fishermen to preach the Gospel in many languages on the day the Church was born.

He bent the rules out of love when He allowed me (and you) into His family.

He bent the rules out of love when He allowed me (and you) another day—this very day—to once again arise from bed and struggle toward His Kingdom.

And, God help me, I pray that when I stand before the Father as judge, instead of looking at my poor record, He'll look upon His Son and, again, bend the rules out of love.

After all, He bent the rules out of love when He allowed that persecutor, Paul, to spread the Faith far and wide.

He bent the rules out of love when He helped an infamous prostitute to be transformed into St. Mary of Egypt, and a thief and murderer to be known as St. Moses the Black.

He bent the rules out of love when, to the guilty thief hanging beside Him, He said, "Today you'll be with Me in Paradise."

Out of love, God bends the rules.

He still does.

That's the way Love is.

That's the rule.

Then again, you probably knew that already. When *I* finally learn it, I will, no doubt, check it off my list.

Expect a Miracle!

That was the way the old Oral Roberts television show began back when I was growing up. Oral's son, Richard, and other snazzy-looking young guys and gals would rush out on stage and, before breaking into song, they would pump up the groggy Sunday TV audience with the challenge, "Expect a miracle!"

During the Ask Abouna sessions one summer at Camp St. Raphael (which, coincidentally, is convened near the home of Oral Roberts University), many of the kids' questions and concerns were the same as every year for that age Christians: "Tell us about demons," and "Why don't miracles happen any more?"

In my experience with church youth groups, though styles and fashions change, the concerns remain the same: Tell us about demons, tell us about miracles. We're always searching, particularly in our youth, for the extraordinary, the mysterious, the powerful; anything to get beyond our mundane existence. Let's start with the miracles; we'll save the demons for last.

Years ago, I had the occasion to attend a Sunday service at a Pentecostal church, a Four Square church. The visit was mainly due to a dare of sorts. Some friends and I, teenagers, happened upon a woman behind the counter in a convenience store who, rightly sensing that we were up to no good, took it upon herself to pray with us—in tongues! She invited us to church with her the next day, and lo and behold—we were young, we were foolish—we went. This was rural North Carolina, mind you; we were all college-aged Protestants. So, forgive me, church hopping was "allowed."

This little Four Square church was packed with people; it only seated a hundred or so, not too big, but the preacher had a microphone and the speakers were turned way up. The organ would play along, for effect, with his preaching.

One of the strangest things was the so-called prophecy phase of the service, wherein a woman would stand up in the back of the church and speak in tongues. (Forgive me here, but it sounded something like, "I-bought-a-Toyota-when-I-shoulda-bought-a-Honda.") Over on the other side of the church another woman would interpret, in Southern twang, "Someone here today is suffering with lower back pain." Sure enough, a man stood up and tearfully exclaimed that it was he! Prayers were said over him and all the people said, "Amen!" (I guess he felt better.)

The woman speaking in tongues continued, "Sheby-shameka-malkutheka . . . who-stolla-my-Honda!" And, punctuated by holy howls from the preacher and the faithful, the interpreter would say, "Someone here is suffering greatly over a wayward daughter." With little hesitation, a woman stood and tearfully admitted it was she. Prayers were said, God was praised (rather, yelled at), and they moved on to the next malady. It was sort of a combination of religion, Oprah, Jerry Springer, and Black Oak Arkansas. Let me explain.

Years ago, back when I was twelve, my parents took a friend and me to a rock concert in Charlotte with some big-name bands and artists: The Four Tops, Charlie Daniels, Gallery, Johnny Nash, and Billy Preston. The final act was a very noisy rock band named Black Oak Arkansas (think "banging gong, clanging cymbal"—minus the love part). As far as I could tell, they too were speaking in tongues!

Anyway, they pranced on stage ranting and raving, barefoot and shirtless; hairy men in spandex pants. I was shocked. Seeing as how I was with my parents, my shock was magnified. After the opening number, the lead singer—a cat called "Jim Dandy"—said, "People call us animals. They say we're wild, untamed—nasty." The crowd, save for me and my parents, was going crazy in hypnotic agreement. "Well, brothers and sisters, we're *not* animals!" And, to the roar of guitar and crowd, he proclaimed, "We're all alike!" That's when my dad said, "Come on, I ain't like him, let's get out of here."

There I sat, a few years later, at the Pentecostal worship service, with prophecies in tongues, interpretations, medical diagnosis, ranting in the microphone, Wurlitzer punctuation marks, and . . . "Uncle Ernie." Uncle Ernie sat—well, stood—up on the front row. He was every bit of 92 years old, and he kept wigglin' and movin', a-hoppin' and a-jumpin'. The pastor, still working the crowd into a frenzy like a spirit-filled auctioneer, cried, "Oh, look at Uncle Ernie! His leg done caught the spirit!"

All you had to do was look at Uncle Ernie to see that his right leg was just a-wigglin' abnormally, out of control. Imagine Elvis, skinny at 92, with one frog leg, one human. The pastor kept up the excitement, saying, "Yes, Lord! Ol' Uncle Ernie's leg is praising the Lord! Soon he'll be runnin' around the building!"

Y'all. Would you believe it? That old man took off and ran clean out of the church! You may be thinking, "Did he really run around the building?" Yes! Thanks to the clear windows of the church, we could see Uncle Ernie running like a madman around the building as the service continued. There's people weeping, there's women screaming, people are speaking in tongues; there's the preacher in a pale blue suit with a black tie and hair tonic screeching into the microphone, and yep, there he goes again. Uncle Ernie kept on circling that little church building. It was a wild and far cry from my boring old Baptist church.

That's when the preacher announced that there were special visitors present and he was going to have them come up to the microphone. I hoped to God he wasn't referring to me and my friends. Nope. There were some missionaries there and, as they approached the microphone, I noticed they were carefully carrying a shoebox.

The preacher said they'd brought a special visitor today (given the excited murmurings of the churchgoers, one who had been with them before). He said the missionaries had, once again, brought back a special visitor named Ralph.

Now friends, when you're in the rural South, at a Pentecostal service, with all sorts of spirit-filled mayhem happening—people are fallin' out* and old Uncle Ernie's sprinting around the building—and then, the preacher invites some visitors up with a shoe box containing a famous visitor named Ralph—well, it can only mean one thing. I looked out the window and spotted Uncle Ernie sprinting around the building and thought to myself, "Dear God in heaven, if they break out a snake, I'm pretty sure I'm gonna catch the spirit, too! You talk about shoutin'! They ain't never heard no shoutin' like I'm gonna be doin' if they spring a snake from that box! Uncle Ernie, here I come!"

In the end, long story short, it was just a hand puppet, not a viper. To tell the truth, after the long build-up—glossolalia, prophecy, Uncle Ernie's antics and all—it was a bit of a letdown.

Now, back to the miracles query. I must admit—and this will make me sound old—but when fresh-faced teens look at me in a group setting and ask, "Why don't miracles happen any more?" I want to say, "You *are* a miracle!" But that would never work; maybe some day when those boys are found standing by their wife's side in the delivery room they'll appreciate it. Maybe after a few bumps and bruises such as most lives suffer, those teens will come to realize that the God of miracles is not a God of second chances but, lo and behold, through repentance, God is infinitely loving and merciful. (Heck, I always thought it a miracle that my dad didn't kill me while I was growing up. But that's another story.)

I know what the teens are asking, perhaps not so much about raising the dead—but their questions were really: "Why aren't my prayers answered?" "Why do people die?" "Where is God in all this?" Those are good questions—nay, better questions than, "Why don't miracles happen any more?"

It's true, from time to time there are signs and wonders made

* Fainting.

manifest, such as weeping icons, incorrupt or fragrant relics, astounding answers to prayers for healing. But normally, God acts normally. *Normally, God acts normally.* Now your mileage may vary with that statement, yet I believe it's true. The thing is, God's normal is not our normal. (And it's way different from what Black Oak Arkansas defined as normal.)

In fact, sometimes—most often—miracles happen, but everything *looks* perfectly normal. A man and a woman stand before the priest and the gathered faithful; they look the same after the prayers as they did before, but by the grace of God the Holy Spirit, they are transformed—changed—to husband and wife, united by God in one flesh.

That man (or woman) looks just the same before confession as after absolution. But by the grace of the Holy Spirit, he is forgiven; his sins are wiped away. Though he resembles that same sinner that sought His mercy just moments before, he is a new creature in Christ.

Then there's the greatest miracle of all—one that literally raises the dead: that little piece of bread and that cup of wine. After the prayers of priest and people, by the wondrous action of the Holy Spirit, that bread and wine still look like plain ol' bread and wine. Yet, glory to God, they are transformed into the very Body and Blood of Christ our God.

Oh, and it gets even better! When we commune, when we receive the Body and Blood of Christ our God, we are changed. We are continually changed through participation in the grace of the Holy Spirit—transformed, as St. Paul says, from glory to glory. This is why we can call each other brothers and sisters—not, as Jim Dandy put it, because we are all animals. Rather, because we all have the same blood flowing through our veins, the blood of Christ, which we receive from the chalice.

This Communion in what appears (normally God acts normally) to be simply bread and wine is what the Church Fathers call the "medicine of immortality." It cures what ails ya. And the common ailment for us all is sin and death. Just as our first parents, Adam and Eve, partook of the forbidden fruit in disobedience and brought forth the bitter fruit of sin and death, the New Adam, Christ our God (only-begotten Son of the Father), bids us toward obedience as we sing, "Receive the Body of Christ, taste the fountain of immortality." Truly, this is an indescribable miracle. That is, if we believe.

Now, on to the demons: yes, they exist. But the main difference between them and the holy angels—the *only* difference—is that they rebelled against God. They chose a different path, away from God, eternally. Misery loves company, and truth be known, those demons will never find happiness, even if you do fall and join them!

When you find yourself tempted by them—when you find yourself in the presence of those who reject God, or stuck in a lifestyle of misery, rejection, and disbelief—you might just be suffering the company of demons. Be like my dad and say, "Come on, I ain't like them, let's get out of here."

The next time you participate in confession, a wedding, a baptism, chrismation, or attend Liturgy, don't look for bells and whistles, tongues and signs, or the churchified version of Jim Dandy ranting like an animal. But do expect a miracle. Because God—well, normally, God acts normally.

Jesus Loves You (But)

My teenaged daughter is, by default, a Priest's Kid (or PK for short). A while back, on a retreat down in the border town of Pharr, Texas, she met another PK, and they became long-distance friends.

Recently, she told me of a T-shirt this girl and some other PKs were marketing that featured, on the front in big letters: "P. K." On the back it read, "We believe because we HAVE to!" Of course, pretending to be a sober-minded daddy priest, I said, "Uh, no." But, really, believing because you *have to* is not such a bad deal.

Life gets a lot more difficult when we grow up and get out on our own and are responsible for our own beliefs. Scarier still is the thought that we will someday be judged not so much by what we said we believed—but by those works which, by God's grace, we did according to that belief.

The saints themselves were not infallible. They, too, were sinners—strugglers just as we are. On this side of hagiography, we tend to remember, and rightly so, the virtues of the saints. Yet during their earthly lives, there were those who knew them differently. There's a saying: "Eternal rest with the saints, *but* you wouldn't want to live with them."

But is a great and disappointing word, depending on context. It can be a temptation, using the word *but*. Sinner that I am, I've often been known to use the word in an apology:

"Listen, I'm really sorry, *but* . . ."

"Forgive me, you know, I was wrong, *but* . . ."

Of course, that word—and what follows it—sort of negates the apology.

"Honey, you've prepared a wonderful dinner, *but . . .*"

"Thank you! I really appreciate it, *but . . .*"

"Yes, we had a good time, *but . . .*"

"You. Look. Lovely tonight, *but . . .*"

Believe me: Those *buts* won't save you.

Parents are very familiar with the word:

"But Dad . . ."

"But Mom . . ."

BUT, but, **but** . . .

Many of you, myself included, have sat across the desk from an important man and heard these words: "Your resumé is impressive, and we'd love to have someone like you on our team, *but . . .*"

Or: "Hey! Congratulations! You almost made it to first place, *but . . .*"

A couple of years ago, a few adults and some wee volunteers were busy stuffing plastic Easter eggs with candy and goodies. That is, most of them were. One creatively naughty little boy was stuffing them with something else. That would be shrimp tails. And that would be . . . my boy.

It was the Wednesday before Lazarus Saturday, the day on which the annual egg hunt is held at St. George Church, Houston. Following the Presanctified Liturgy, some folks helped to stuff the eggs for the following Saturday. It was after the Lenten potluck, hence the shrimp. Dead shrimp, dead shrimp tails, stuffed in plastic eggs, to sit for three days, hidden and undiscovered, until found by some unsuspecting happy children. *Priceless.* Oh, don't get me wrong, he was wrong! *But* I was kind of proud of him.

I remember when my oldest was about four years old. It was after church one day, and the kids were running around the yard, climbing trees, and creating mayhem. I was talking with some parishioners when I happened to look off in the distance to see a boy, about the same age as my daughter, holding her down and, *gasp,* kissing her!

I walked out and called his name, yelling, "Hey! Get off of her!" Almost at the same time could be heard the voice of the boy's dad, yelling, "That's my boy! Heh heh, yep! That's my boy!" For him, it was priceless; *but* for me, not so much.

It's all in perception. And when perception is viewed through the favoring eyes of love, it looks a whole shade different. Love of my daughter led me to yell one thing; his hopes and love for his son caused an entirely different reaction.

Love definitely complicates things, but you just can't simplify without it. St. Paul writes:

> Though I speak with the tongues of men and of angels, but have not love, I have become sounding brass or a clanging cymbal. And though I have the gift of prophecy, and understand all mysteries and all knowledge, and though I have all faith, so that I could remove mountains, but have not love, I am nothing. And though I bestow all my goods to feed the poor, and though I give my body to be burned, but have not love, it profits me nothing.
>
> Love suffers long and is kind; love does not envy; love does not parade itself, is not puffed up; does not behave rudely, does not seek its own, is not provoked, thinks no evil; does not rejoice in iniquity, but rejoices in the truth; bears all things, believes all things, hopes all things, endures all things. Love never fails. (1 Corinthians 13:1–8a)

Now, back to my boy—*boy* being the operative word here: You've got to admit, that was a great trick—stinky ol' shrimp tails inside hidden plastic eggs. When he knew that I knew, he was scared. He thought I'd be mad at him. When I brought it up, he started to cry. He was shocked when I held out my hand and said, "Give me five!" Laughter through young tears is priceless. (Oh, don't worry, the tails were discovered and discarded long before the cherished children's event.)

And so it goes. When we don't love someone, we find no joy in anything they say or do. Yet love covers a multitude of sins.

> For now we see in a mirror, dimly, but then face to face.
> Now I know in part, but then I shall know just as I also am
> known. And now abide faith, hope, love, these three; but
> the greatest of these is love. (1 Corinthians 13:12–13)

Love, thanks to God, never ends.

Later that same year, the year of the Easter-egg-shrimp-tails, the kids had returned from church camp, a ten-hour bus trip. My son had fallen asleep and—*welcome to kid camp travel*—some kid had drawn on his face with markers. (Aren't you glad you're grown?) Anyway, when he awoke to find out, he was mad. He stayed mad, even telling me about it, until he discovered that the markings were not the work of a suspected little boy, but of his own sister and her girlfriends. Again, it's all in perception. And when anything is viewed through the favoring eyes of love, it looks a whole shade different.

Which brings me back to *but*. Notice the Scripture verse (above) doesn't say, "Love never ends, *but* . . ." Those *buts*, the ones we continually use, those *buts* won't save you. At the Last Day, when we stand before our Lord and Judge: no buts.

"You see, Lord, I would have helped the poor, *but* I thought it better that they help themselves . . ."

Or: "I know I should have visited those in prison, *but* frankly those kinds of people disgust me. Besides, I didn't know anybody there . . ."

Or: "I could have done better, really I could, *but* I saw something on Oprah . . ."

This all sounds like the man in the parable with the one talent:

> "Then he who had received the one talent came and said,
> 'Lord, I knew you to be a hard man, reaping where you

have not sown, and gathering where you have not scattered seed. And I was afraid, and went and hid your talent in the ground. Look, there you have what is yours.'" (Matthew 25:24–25)

So, you see, this side of the grave or the other, *buts* won't save us.

But remember what I said about perception? It's all in perception. And when anything is viewed through the favoring eyes of love, it looks a whole shade different. Thus, there is one instance I can imagine when that word, *but*, might just work. When that day comes, as we stand to be judged, there's certain to be many accusations flying about. Our constant companions and false judges, the demons, will yell:

She was an adulterer!
He was a mean man!
Him? He was a thief!
Her? She thought only of herself!
He liked to drink! She liked to curse!
These two, they broke a vow!

And so forth. Until, pay attention, here it comes: *BUT*. When that one voice rings out: "*But*," says the Lord, "these are Mine!" the devil, our accuser, will be silenced.

Until that great and terrible day, let us believe, not because your daddy's a priest, but because our great God and Savior has destroyed death and opened the way to Paradise for all who believe in Him. Let us believe because we have to.

When our Lord, the all-merciful Savior, says, "*But*, Satan be gone, these whom you have vexed and accused—these are Mine!" there will be no more *buts*. The enemy will be silenced. Silenced—by the big *but* of mercy.

Theological BS

These days, no matter the price of gasoline, most of us spend a lot of time in our cars, on the road. Which means—you can't always be the leader—we're often following somebody.

Back in high school, thirty years ago, I had a bumper sticker on my car that read, "Honk if you love Willie Nelson." Yes, it's true, I did. Picture a 1978 Camaro Z-28 with the sticker, "Honk if you love Willie Nelson."

But, silly me, I always seemed to forget the sticker was there. It happened that every now and then, while I was stopped at a red light or stop sign, or the traffic was moving slowly, someone would blow their horn at me—and I would get so mad!

Frederica Mathewes-Green once dreamed of a bumper sticker that said, "Honk 40 times if you're Orthodox." No doubt, that would have driven me to road rage! Thing is, if you're *really* Orthodox, you'd have three of those stickers on your car; devoted followers would have to honk 120 times—even more with a *Dynamis* thrown in!

I believe Tony Orlando, of Tony Orlando and Dawn fame (also thirty years ago), is responsible for today's popular bumper stickers: you know, the looped ribbons of different colors that say "Support our Troops" or "Fight Breast Cancer" or what have you. It all began when they sang, "Tie a yellow ribbon 'round the old oak tree . . ."

Then there's the obligatory magnetic fish symbol some Christians put on their car, which, of course, evolved into a magnetic fish with feet in honor of, good grief, Charles Darwin's theory of evolution. Oh, but then there's the one that shows the magnetic fish swallowing the Darwin fish, sort of a survival-of-the-fittest-magnetic-fish, Jesus style.

Orthodox Christianity, thank goodness, doesn't lend itself very well to bumper sticker theology. Sure, you can see Orthodox Christians with those magnetic fishies or a window decal featuring a cross. But the more popular version of so-called Christian bumper stickers is far from Orthodox theology.

There's that sticker that reads, "Next time you think you're perfect, try walking on water." Talk about snarky! Forget Peter, I always think of St. Mary of Egypt when I read that one.

A few years ago you saw these: "Hate is not a family value." I always wondered how the person sporting that one defined *family*; differently from me, I guessed. Then again, they probably defined *hate* differently, too. Ultimately, I think they just needed a hug. Better yet, a rewording a la P.D. Eastman: "Do you like my hate? I do not like your hate. Goodbye."

In the hipper hills of Western North Carolina, one often sees a bumper sticker saying, "Love Your Mother"—with an image of the earth. I always wanted to make some that say, "Love Your Mother"—with an image of the Theotokos.

When Kinky Friedman ran for governor of Texas, there were quirky bumper stickers everywhere; one said, "My Governor Is a Jewish Cowboy." This was, of course, a spin on the ol' "My Boss Is a Jewish Carpenter" stickers. Being a bumper sticker reactionary, I always had problems with that one. First off, the Lord is not a boss; He undoubtedly hails from the House of David, but to say He's a Jewish carpenter? (Come to think of it, no offense intended here: Have you ever met an actual *Jewish* carpenter? That would change Handel's whole *Messiah*: "Wonderful! *Carpenter!* Almighty God!")

No doubt, you've seen the one that says, "In case of rapture this car will be unmanned." But have you seen my favorite—"In case of rapture, may I have your car?"

How 'bout "God Is My Co-Pilot"? *Co*-pilot? Hello! That tempts me to create one saying, "Mary Is My Co-Pilot."

A couple of Christmases ago, a car passed me with a sticker saying, "Jesus Is the Reason for the Season." Honestly, I hadn't gone two miles before a contrary message appeared at a church: "Jesus Is the Gift, YOU Are the Reason."

Ah, yes, church reader boards:

God may say WAIT
But He never says WORRY.

Get rich quick—
Count your blessings!

Exposure to the SON
May Prevent Burning.

Then there are those that are specific to one's locality. Here in Texas there's a saying: *Never stare at the driver of the car with the bumper sticker that says, "Keep honking, I'm reloading."* In Houston, there's a host of sayings, like:

Forget the traffic rules you learned elsewhere. Houston has its own version of traffic rules: Hold on and pray.

There is no such thing as a dangerous high-speed chase in Houston. We all drive like that.

If you actually stop at a yellow light, you will be rear-ended, cussed out, and possibly shot. When you are the first one off the starting line, count to five when the light turns green before going, to avoid getting into any cross-traffic's way.

Or, as one shop-keep told me, "In Houston, red lights mean nothing." And that, my friends, is, unfortunately, *absolutely* true!

One day, after leaving a downtown hospital, I was following a small slow-moving red car. Seeing that there was a glaring red light up ahead, I could tell the driver was not planning to stop. I slowed down a bit and, much as if I was watching a movie, the following scene occurred: The little red car sailed right through the red light, and from its left came a man driving a green van, 40 mph, windows down, minding his own business and the rules of the road. *BAM!* The red car hit the green van in just such a way as to send it into the air, flipping it. It smashed into the sidewalk, only feet from a pedestrian, and rolled over until it was upright and catty-corner in the road. For a few seconds, time stood still.

WOW.

I got out of my car and, as if in a dream, made my way toward the two vehicles. A woman emerged from the small red car; she was okay. I didn't know what I would find in the green van. But, to my amazement, there sat a man with a scrape or two on his arm, but otherwise okay! (No, he did not have his seatbelt on.)

Both the woman who'd hit him, and the man whose van had tumbled through the street, started thanking God. True, I was dressed as a priest, but I don't think I can take the credit.

As I was talking to him, there at the crossroads, I noticed a dead wasp lying flat on its back on the man's dashboard. Also, some bits of Fritos and broken pieces of crayon littered his dashboard, along with quite a bit of dust. I thought to myself, "That's odd." How could those tiny objects stay in place on his dashboard as he drives down the road with his windows down?

Then it occurred to me: They're not normally there. These are all things that are usually hidden from view, under seats and in crevices. Yet today, when he came to the crossroads, his life was literally turned upside down. What was usually hidden was suddenly revealed.

And, though it'll probably sound corny, I thought to myself, "This is what sometimes happens at the *Cross*roads. When we encounter Christ, our lives are turned upside down, and much of what was previously hidden in darkness is revealed in the light. Through a tumultuous experience, we end up praising God. If nothing else, we are changed."

Come to think of it, I believe it was John the Baptist who came up with the perfect bumper sticker: "Repent, for the Kingdom of God is at hand!" Think about it. You gotta admit, that's a great bumper sticker. What else need be said? "Repent, for the Kingdom of God is at hand!"

It should not be taken as a dire and scary warning; repentance is not merely a matter of rummaging around in our personal sins, engaging in self-flagellation, and trying to uncover and expose as much inner evil, dirt, and darkness as possible. Even the devil can help you dig up dirt on yourself! Rather, true repentance is more connected with light than darkness, with the awesome mystery of God's mercy more than with our dark and evil deeds.

To truly repent, we must turn from the darkness to the light. This is done especially when we recognize God's mercy and forgiveness—and how truly unworthy we are. When standing before God as He truly is, we weep at our shabby and unworthy selves. This brings about amendment of life, new life, through His Son, Christ our Lord. Following this, true repentance is reflected more in our deeds than in our thoughts or words. True repentance is born in our putting off the old self-centered man and putting on the new man in Christ. This bears fruit in our helping our neighbor.

The woman who hit the man? She was so very sorry, yet praising God that they both were alive. The man who'd stared at death right then and there and only came away with scrapes? Though his vehicle was ruined, he was profoundly grateful; I'm sure he was seeing life through a new set of eyes. It mattered not one whit that he'd had trash under his seat which was now exposed. He was alive!

Had the accident been avoided, or had it been more normal, a near miss, there would have, no doubt, been honking of horns, muttering of curses, and well, just plain sin. Yet that day, at the crossroads near St. Joseph's Hospital, two people's lives were changed, I can't help but believe for the better.

Be careful out there. Remember the guy in front of you, the one beside you, and the one in your rearview mirror in your prayers.

And, no matter what bumper stickers you may see, think about the one you probably won't:

> *Repent, for the Kingdom of God is at hand!*
> ***Repent, for the Kingdom of God is at hand!***

Oh—and, no matter what or whom their bumper sticker claims to love, don't honk at anyone. (Besides, everyone in Texas loves Willie Nelson.)

Part IV

Just Gimme That
Ol' Country Religion

Bless Your Heart—
Smallah, Smallah, Smallah!

I've never been good with languages. For example, I once worked with a fellow who was fluent in German. One day, he sneezed. I said, "Gesundheit."

He said, "Why did you say that?"

"Well, I thought it meant 'God bless you' or 'Good health' or something like that."

He said, "Everyone thinks that. It actually means, 'Oh, you sneezed.'" (I later found out he was teasing, of course.)

These days, I'm trying to learn some Arabic; like, "Good morning!"—*Sabah al khair*. And the reply: *Sabah al nur*. Like, in the South, we say, "Hire you?" And the reply: "Fine you?"

Imagine my surprise when I approached a man from Ramallah and said, "*Sabah al khair!*" And he replied, "Oh, you sneezed!"

Okay, so I made that part up. But America is a big and complex country, made up mostly of people who came from somewhere else. And this gets really quirky when you mix Orthodox Christianity in with the cultural peculiarities of *The South*. Now, when I say *The South*, I am referring to that region formerly referred to as the Confederacy. And, for reality's sake, one must admit that Florida's been annexed by New York, portions of Virginia resemble Washington, DC, and Texas is, let's be real, a country unto itself.

Nonetheless, the question arises: Orthodoxy—*in the South*? To illustrate, let's run through a Top Ten List:

You Know You're Southern Orthodox When:

10. At Pentecost, your church is decorated with kudzu.

9. You spell "feast" with only three letters: B B Q.

8. You say "Father," "Barsanuphios," and "Monastery" without pronouncing an "r".

7. You drive three hours to an Orthodox church. But you could hop on one foot, with your eyes closed and a rock in your shoe, to the nearest Baptist church.

6. Your services are all in English—at least that's what *you* call it.

5. There are women in your church known as Photini Beth, Thecla Beth, and Elizabeth Beth.

4. There are men going by Athanasius Lee, Euphrosynos Lee, and Vasiliy Lee.

3. You've got white folks, black folks—even Democrats—in your parish, but no Russians, Serbians, Arabs, or Greeks.

2. You know someone who knows someone who knows someone with a velvet picture of Elvis celebrating the Last Supper.

AND—the number one sign that you are an Orthodox Southerner:

1. *You think grits are too good to be considered fasting!*

But, in all honesty, though there are cultural differences within this ethnic soup we call Orthodoxy, we're not as different as it appears. We just use different words to say similar things. For example, in *The South* we say, "Bless your heart." Someone once said, "A true Southerner knows you don't scream obscenities at little old ladies who drive 30 miles per hour on the freeway; you just say, 'Bless her heart' and go your own way."

Then again, by adding that Southern phrase—"Bless your heart"—you can say pretty much anything you want. "Oh, look at her; she's put on so much weight. Bless her heart." "He is so lazy, bless his heart." "And ugly! Bless his heart." Well, you get the picture.

This brings me to the evil eye. The belief in the evil eye is common to most Mediterranean and Middle Eastern countries, regardless of education, religion, or urban/rural context. In the Middle East, it is part and parcel of everyday life. The eye is cast by a person, most often involuntarily and unconsciously, through envy or jealousy. So, for instance, a Middle Eastern lady sees a cute little girl and gushes, "She's so cute! Ohh. *Smallah, smallah, smallah!*" First glimpse of that newborn baby? *Smallah, smallah, smallah!* The bride in her bridal gown? *Smallah, smallah, smallah!* The groom in his ill-fitting tux? *Bless his heart.*

Smallah—which means "In the name of God"—is a beautiful habit to protect against the sin of envy. "Bless your heart" is a quirky little prayer, of sorts, to soften hard reality.

In other words, to avoid casting the eye, Middle Easterners will add *Smallah* ("In the name of God") when they are complimenting someone's children or possessions. When someone showers you with compliments, you may jokingly say, "Stop or you'll hit me with the eye!" A consequence of this belief is that Lebanese are accustomed not to speak of projects that aren't securely founded yet, lest they be affected.

No different in *The South*; for instance, "Hush your mouth." My mom would often say this to me whenever I spoke of some horrible worry or the potential for future disaster: "Hush your mouth, son" (as if my saying it might just make it happen).

My point is, dig deeply enough and we're all the same: the same struggles, the same joys, the same sorrows, the same need. We all need salvation. And to achieve that salvation we not only need God, we also need each other. We need the Church. The Church is made up of nothing but sinners—no matter your ethnicity, no matter your language, social status, or particular illness.

Our Lord said (in Aramaic), "Go, make disciples of *all* nations." And, *nuschur Allah* (Arabic: "Thanks be to God"), this is happening— even in Texas, Florida, Virginia, and *The South*. It is no longer foreign: Orthodoxy. Rather, by God's grace and the patient endurance of those who came before us, the ancient Faith, once lived primarily by Russians, Serbians, Arabs, and Greeks, is being joyfully embraced by rednecks, plow jocks, and city folk; not only in the Bible Belt but in the Heartland, the Great Lakes, the Northwest & the Sandwich Islands. *Smallah, Smallah, Smallah.*

Malo pomalo (Russian: "little by little"), by God's grace, we toil in this vineyard. "Baptizing them in the name of the Father and the Son and the Holy Spirit," and, our Lord continues, "I am with you always—even to the end of the age."

How do we bring Americans to Orthodoxy? It takes time. It takes patience. It takes perseverance. It takes translators! It takes love, forgiveness, and understanding. We all need each other, struggling together within the Church.

I once heard a pal relate the story of his getting a speeding ticket, whereupon he asked the officer, "Look at all those cars speeding past. Out of all these, why me?" The patrolman looked at him, smiled, and said, "Did you ever go fishing?" And before my friend could answer, he continued, "Did you ever catch them all?"

The same held true even for our Lord and the apostles. Alas, not everyone—bless their hearts—will come home to the True Faith. As they say in *The South*, "You can't make a silk purse out of a sow's ear." *Inchallah* (Arabic: "Good Lord willing and the creek don't rise"), *malo pomalo*, we'll make it. Nonetheless, as St. John Chrysostom was wont to say, and this works well in any language: "Glory to God for all things."

He's in a Better Place . . . Than Dixie?

....

We hear it from time to time: a silly thing, really. Truth be known, we've all probably said it: "He (or she) is in a better place." And if you've said it before, forgive me; I'm not criticizing you. Lord knows *I've* probably even said it.

Sometimes when we try to comfort someone who has just lost a loved one, we say he or she is in a better place. I don't *think* it's just a Southern thing, though it could be. But we'll come back to that in a moment.

For now, while I'm at it, let me take a wide turn here in regard to *place*. I mean, everyone's from somewhere, and we can't really help that. Your mom, your dad, they just happened to be living somewhere when you were born and raised and, *voila*, that place becomes part of you.

The thing about being a Southern native, especially with a podcast, website, and email address using the word *Dixie*, is: Some folks make assumptions about you—a negative sort of profiling, if you will. Not all folks think this way; these days, lots of folks think being Southern is cool. But to paraphrase an old Barbara Mandrell song: "I was Dixie when Dixie wasn't cool."

And in passing—just for the record—about the corruption of the word *Orthodoxy* into *Orthodixie*, at least my story (realizing that other people use the word these days) is this: When we were on the way to converting to Orthodoxy years ago, a young man (now known as "Fr. Paul the Monk" or Monk Paul Hagiopavlites) and I were on our way to St. Ignatius Orthodox Church in Franklin, Tennessee. We were laughing about a lot of things, discovering Orthodoxy can be quite fun, and I used the word *Orthodixie* to describe us: two Southern boys, raised Baptist, on our way to Orthodoxy—in my case, the priesthood, and in his, monasticism.

Later that same trip, we saw Fr. Gordon Walker's son, Tom, give a concert at St. Ignatius—sort of a country-Christian-convert-meets-Constantinople concert—and I later told Fr. Gordon that we'd dubbed his son's music "Orthodixie." We all laughed. When the Internet came into vogue, and it came time to come up with an email address, I chose *Orthodixie* as my handle and, well, there it is.

Also, while we're near the subject, let's talk about profiling. I think about profiling a lot during the Paschal season.

When someone who looks Arab comes up to kiss the cross, I say, "*Al Maseeh Qam!*"

If they look Greek: "*Christos Anesti!*"

If they look Russian: "*Christos Voskrese!*"

If they look like just plain ol' white folks, I say, "Happy Easter!"

I'm just kidding! As I always put in our parish's Pascha bulletin:

> During the forty days of Pascha, it is customary to begin all correspondence (letters and email) and all conversations (phone and in person) with "Christ is Risen!" The response is "Indeed, He is Risen!" or "Truly, He is Risen!" This may be done in a variety of languages, none of which sound anything like "Happy Easter!"

Anyway . . . A couple years back, having just returned to Houston from my home state of North Carolina, I thought back to how amazingly overgrown with vegetation the Ol' North State is; compared to Houston, even the more urban areas of North Carolina look way too green. (That's a good thing.)

And nuthin' could be finer than the accents in Carolina. Just plain cool! Like others with a spare twang, I can polish mine up and sound like the rest when surrounded by the best. (Okay, so I couldn't hide mine if I tried. But you know what I mean.)

Those two weeks back in North Carolina coincided with two weeks around living television sets. Other than an occasional program via rabbit ears, we don't watch TV in the Huneycutt house. So I thank God that this opportunity is rare. While channel surfing, I had the misfortune to hear a country song by Hank Williams, Jr., "That's How We Do It in Dixie!" accompanied by the music video. Y'all, that ain't how decent folks do it in Dixie. (I'll bet ol' Hank don't even do it that way!)

Though a Southerner, I just can't relate to country songs like Hank Williams, Jr.'s:

If heaven ain't a lot like Dixie, I don't wanna go.
If heaven ain't a lot like Dixie, I'd just as soon stay home.

Or Tanya Tucker's:

When I die I may not go to heaven.
I don't know if they let cowboys in.
If they don't, just let me go to Texas,
Boy! Texas is as close as I've been.

No sir. After a night's camping in Everglades National Park in Florida, my dad would say, "If I had a mansion in Florida and a home in hell, I'd sell out and go home." (If you promise not to tell, that's the same way I used to feel about Texas.)

But, as you all know, there are many facets to one's culture, and when we die, well, I don't believe we'll be heading to Dixie, or Delaware, or Missouri, or Alaska, or Chicago. *Inchallah*, the Kingdom! And in the Kingdom, there's room for all: Democrats, rednecks, Roman Catholics, even Yankees. (Wait. How 'bout we settle for three out of four?)

The way I read the Scriptures and understand the teaching of the Church is that God's "profiling" is concerned more with what we *do* out of love than where we're born, whom we voted for, or whether we believe in states' rights or the Western Rite.

We can argue about those, and a host of other topics, but given that we all seek a common Kingdom, we all have the same King. And He plainly states that we are to pray for our enemies, do good to those that hate us, feed the hungry, and clothe the naked—well, you know the drill. In these times of war and chaos, it's nice to be reminded that God is with us, no matter our culture!

But growing up in the rural South, though it was as late as the sixties and seventies, I'm quite familiar with a subject that is now deemed taboo. I'm talking about [*whisper*]: *segregation*. To be perfectly honest, it's not a bad thing, segregation. I have no idea what you're thinking about, but I'm talking about women in the kitchen and men in the den!

At an early age, I learned that if you really want to know anything about anybody, you had to hang out with the women in the kitchen. Besides, the conversations with the men in the den often go like this: "ZZZZZZZZZZZZZZZzzzzzzzzzzzzzzzzzzzzzzz . . ."

But the info, the business—*everybody's* business—was all the buzz in the kitchen. Little pitchers have big ears, but pitchers go unnoticed in the kitchen. When you get a little older—that is, if you are a male—the business ain't so newsy when you're around. Still, women share an innate sense of togetherness that transcends anything the opposite sex shares naturally.

In the Gospel for the second Sunday after Pascha, we read about the *women* who went to the tomb early in the morning to anoint the body of Jesus. Jesus had been hastily buried in a tomb owned by Joseph of Arimathea with the help of the other secret disciple, Nicodemus. These two men, Joseph of Arimathea and Nicodemus, are included in the full list of myrrhbearers, but generally this day is understood as the Sunday of the Myrrhbearing *Women*.

Of the remaining eleven disciples, *all men*, not one of them is listed as a myrrhbearer. The men who had followed when He said,

"Come, follow Me"—the men who appear throughout the Gospel narratives—those men? All, save one, abandoned Him after the Crucifixion.

Now here we see a band of women disciples making their way toward the tomb with only God knew what awaiting them. Did you ever wonder what those myrrhbearing women were talking about? I mean, the Gospel plainly says they were talking to each other on the way to the tomb (Mark 16:3). Do you think, to comfort each other in their grief, they said, "He's in a better place"? Can you imagine? Jesus of Nazareth dies and His followers say, "Oh well, He's in a better place." How silly.

When our Lord and His disciples came upon a bier bearing the dead body of the only son of a widow, did our Lord stop the funeral procession and go up to the widow, saying, "Do not cry. He's in a better place"?

When our Lord entered the bedroom of Jairus's daughter along with Peter, James, John, and her parents, was it to console them and say, "You know, really, she's in a better place"?

When He arrived to see His grieving friends Martha and Mary by the tomb of their brother Lazarus, what did He say? "He's in a better place"?

No!

He said to the mother, "Do not weep." And to the dead man: "Young man, I say to you, arise."

He told the dead girl's parents, "The child is not dead, but sleeping." To the girl He said, "Little girl, I say to you, arise." He told the sisters of the dead man, Lazarus, "Your brother will rise again." And to the dead He cried with a loud voice, "Lazarus, come forth!"

Never, not once, is it recorded that our Lord, when faced with the death of a fellow struggler, said, "He's in a better place." And, when you think about it, saying, "He (or she) is in a better place," is just not right. What loved one is going to agree that there's a *better place* than *with them*? You're going to tell a mom, a dad, or sisters that their departed loved one is in a better place?

No.

That's not what our Lord said. He said, "Get up. Death has no more dominion over you! Arise, I say!" Because our Lord knows that the best place for anyone to be is with the people who love him. Let me repeat: Our Lord knows that the best place for anyone to be is with the people who love her!

Look around you: you don't love the people you see? Careful, cause you might not like heaven. If we relish being separated from our brothers, especially Christians, in this life, we probably aren't registered for that heavenly mansion in the next.

Speaking of which: Those women arrived at the tomb to find it empty, and in God's choosing to announce the Resurrection through the daughters of Eve, the Holy Myrrhbearers, we see the Annunciation in another light. Whereas earlier, a young maiden had heard the words of the archangel Gabriel in private, here, an angel announces to the Mother of God and faithful women disciples the Resurrection. The way to Paradise has been reopened, for our Lord has destroyed death by death. Go! Announce to the sons of Adam the New Day, the Resurrection.

Today the New Eve hears that her Son, the New Adam, has conquered death by His glorious Resurrection and has paved the way for the sons and daughters of the Church—you, me, yours and mine—to enter Paradise!

Elder Paisios of the Holy Mountain gave as good a summary as any. When he was once asked where the soul goes when it leaves the body, he answered, "Well, when the watch stops working, it goes to the hands of the watchmaker. In the same way, our soul goes into the hands of God."

He also said this: "When I see Christians cry because their fathers passed away, I am upset, for they neither believe nor understand that death is simply a journey to life of another kind."

And, to be honest, I don't want that journey to end in Dixie, or Texas, or anywhere but where love is—my loved ones and the One who is Love, who loves me. Returning to where we began:

Everyone's going *somewhere,* and unlike where we're born, we *do* play a role in where we end up. Your departed mom, your dad, sister, brother, or spouse: they are on that mysterious journey. It's only a "better place" if Love is there. Let's pray that includes all of us.

Letters from the Old Country

The Orthodixie headquarters is blessed, from time to time, to receive letters and email from Ancient Faith Radio listeners. Just for fun, here's a few:

Dear Fr. Joseph,

I am new to Orthodoxy, having converted last Pascha, and since that time I've heard the phrase "back in the Old Country" many, many times.

Just what does this mean—the old country—and, I feel stupid asking . . . just where is it?

Lost in Indiana

Dear Lost,

You are closer than you think! For instance, I also come from the Old Country. "North Carolina?" you say. No, Palestine! That's right, though I say I grew up near Charlotte, that really means Albemarle. But that's not exact either, as my boyhood home's mailing address was New London, and just one mile up the road from my house was the closest, though unincorporated, little town: Palestine. Do folks in Palestine, North Carolina, speak a foreign language? You betcha! So, see. Everyone has their own "Old Country."

Actually—come closer, I don't want to say this out loud—but the term "Old Country" refers to a mythical land where everything was so wonderful that, well, in order to increase the struggle toward salvation, it required a move to this country: America.

Because we've currently run out of new places to go, any place other than America will always be the Old Country. Even those who live in the Old Country have to come to the New Country from time to time, in hopes of helping to finance the Old Country.

Hope this helps.

Fr. Joseph

_____

Dear Fr. Joseph,

My sister goes to a church, not an Orthodox church, that is very contemporary and politically correct. They even say the Lord's Prayer beginning with the words "Our Mother, who art in heaven." And, of course, they have a woman priest. Do you see such innovations coming to Orthodoxy?

Sally in San Antonio

_____

Dear Sally,

I don't know how to put this, but I suspect your sister goes to a sissy church. Until she heeds the call to "man up," we'll just have to keep her in our prayers.

The reason our Lord would never have prayed "Our Mother in heaven" is—you ready for this?—listen carefully, and you can quote me on this: it's because His mother wasn't in heaven; she was right down the street!

Unlike fairy tales, which can be rewritten to reflect changes in language and culture (even political correctness), we believe that Jesus is real; His Father was (and is) really in heaven. And in giving the disciples this example of prayer, He was inviting us all to His Father's Kingdom through adoption in Himself!

So, no, we don't pray "Our Mother in heaven . . ." That's just silly.

As to the ordination of women to the priesthood, given the spiritual quagmire brought about by radical feminist ideas which have not, truly, grown up within the Church, but have seduced even some of the brightest minds, we will undoubtedly have to answer this question one day.

But, honestly, only a united Church can speak with a clear and honest voice on such issues (no matter how strong our own personal opinions). Pray for and work toward a unified Church in America. Once we have jurisdictional administrative unity, it will be easier for the haze to be dispelled by clear rain from our Father in heaven, through His holy Church.

Fr. Joseph

─────────

Greetings, Abouna,

I need some clarification.

Like many good people, I receive a plethora of forwarded emails on a daily basis, many of which, during a recent political season, involved politics and the candidates running for election. For instance, some said that George Bush is the devil. Others warned that Barack Obama is the devil. Still others claimed that Sarah Palin is Ol' Scratch.

What say ye?

Tim in Tennessee

─────────

Hi Tim,

Well do I remember that turbulent political season! I also remember lamenting to a fellow seminarian years ago, "Why are there all these battles about whether God's male or female, but the devil's always seen as male?"

"That's her greatest lie!" he replied.

Just kidding. Joe Biden is the boogeyman. *Heh heh.*

Let me tell you a little story. Back when I was a seminarian, I did my internship at a wonderful parish in Asheville, North Carolina: Grace Episcopal Church.

One Sunday I preached a sermon on the Gospel reading about the healing of a man possessed by demons. Several times during the course of the homily, I used the phrase, "Many of you may not believe in demons." At the time, I thought I was really delivering *the word* for these needy hearers.

After the Mass was ended, the pastor asked if he could meet with me in his office. Though he was a gracious and hospitable man, I feared he was offended by my strong and, no doubt, very orthodox message.

"You said in your sermon that 'many do not believe in demons'—well," he said, "that's a good thing; we don't want people to *believe* in demons."

"Unh-huh," I thought, "he's obviously a liberal."

Then he said, "Because when we say we believe in something or someone, that means we place all our trust and hope in that something or someone. Thus, we don't want folks to *believe* in demons or the devil."

I think of that many times when we recite the Creed in church.

No, I don't believe the president, the vice president, or any former candidates are the devil. But I do know that the rebellious angels are constantly at work to divide and destroy. Don't believe in demons! No matter your worldly politics, trust in God. As Psalm 145 says, "Put not your trust in princes or sons of men, in whom there is no salvation."

That said, did you ever wonder who started all those silly emails? This may shock you, but it was none other than Mike Huckabee.

Oh, I'm just kiddin'—it's the devil! *(Scaramouche, Scaramouche, can you do the fandango?)*

That's right, the devil. Just delete 'em!

Cheers!

Fr. Joseph

Dear Fr. Joseph,

A while back, Oxford University released their list of top ten irritating phrases, things like:

➤ *At the end of the day*

➤ *I personally*

➤ *At this moment in time*

➤ *With all due respect*

➤ *And—24/7*

Are there any words or phrases, within Orthodox parlance, that you find irritating?

Sincerely,

Sean in Cheyenne

—————

Dear Sean,

I'm glad you asked. When I was growing up in the Old Country (near Charlotte, near Albemarle, near New London—Palestine—remember?), our preacher would often, at least three times a sermon, use the word *behoove* or *behooves*. As a kid that always caught my ear because I thought it sounded like a dirty word. A preacher saying a dirty word in a Baptist church is something a young boy takes note of! But I digress.

Yes! Chief among irritating phrases used in Orthodoxy is, "The Fathers say . . ."

If your priest says this way too often, it may be a way of saying, "Look, I know you might disagree with me here, so I'm going to blame—I mean *attribute*—the Fathers." Or he might mean, "I read it somewhere, I don't know where, but I think it must have been in the Church Fathers."

If priests are going to quote Church Fathers, it is better for them to actually *name* the Father they are quoting. After all, the Fathers of the Church said many things. (Yet, if they ever said *behoove*, I don't recall.)

Another irritating phrase in Orthodox parlance is, "Do the best you can." Like with fasting, some priests will say, "Just do the best you can." *Hello!* Doing the best I can is what got me in the state I'm in! I need to do better!

Another irritating phrase in Orthodoxy is, "So . . . what led you to become Orthodox?"

After about the 4,392nd time, most converts tire of recounting their journey to Orthodoxy. And, besides, the people that ask the question often get a dazed and uninterested look on their face about 45 seconds into your thrilling conversion story.

So here's what I suggest: Make up something creative. Next time someone asks, "So, what led you to Orthodoxy?" say something like, "The food. No, seriously, you guys have the best food around. No kidding!" (People from the Old Country really like this answer.)

Or say, "Well, you know, in my previous church the services were all in English, and I began to feel so, well, I felt like a sinner. You know? Then I found this church, and I can't understand half the stuff y'all are saying. It must all be about y'all." Heh heh.

On second thought, that might not go over so well.

I remember once, in the Old Country (North Carolina), a parishioner and I were waiting in line for a sandwich at a Subway restaurant. I had a long beard and ponytail and was dressed in a cassock. The fellow wrapping the subs by the cash register, who had tattoos all over his arms and an attitude in his eyes, kept staring at me. I figured he thought *I* was some kind of nut job.

When we got up to his station, he said, "Who ya with?"

I said, "Excuse me?"

"Who you with?" he repeated.

Sheepishly, I said, "I'm an Orthodox Christian priest."

"Oh, humph," he replied.

And that was it. After we got outside, I turned to the parishioner and said, "You know, when he asked 'who ya with?' I should have said something silly like 'Waffle House'." We laughed.

A year or so later, on the way to St. Seraphim Church Camp, another priest and I were eating with the campers in a restaurant in the Old Country (Virginia) and I noticed a woman kept staring at us.

Later, as we stood outside talking, a deacon had joined us—that made three men in black dresses with long hair and beards—and I could see, out of the corner of my eye, this woman and her friends slowly approaching us. We kept talking until I felt a gentle tug at my elbow, and with a wonderful down-home Virginia accent, she said, "Excuse me, but who're y'all with?"

Without blinking I turned to her and said, "Waffle House."

This woman literally lost it! She turned red in the face, burst out laughing, and hit me on the arm, saying, "Now you oughtta be ashamed o' yo'self! I was so nervous—and now you go and say 'Waffle House'—why, I oughtta . . ."

It was funny. So funny, in fact, that I later shared that story with an area "non-denominational" clergy gathering in a local restaurant. About thirty minutes after its telling, a man who had apparently overheard our conversation approached our table and said, "Excuse me, but are you Fr. Joseph?"

I said, "Yes," and he said, "Are you still with Waffle House?"

Ha!

Forgive me,

Fr. Joseph

Well, that's enough about the Old Country. But, brothers and sisters, be of good cheer, for our Lord comes! And when we get to where we're going, this will *all* have been the Old Country! And there will be no one longing to return. We'll all speak the same language, or at least we'll understand them all, and nothing will be lacking except Satan, sin, and death. Though the Old Country's nice, the travel is arduous. It should all prove worthwhile when we get there, though—to the New Country, that is.

When the Roll
Is Called Up Yonder

We were young, in high school, carefree and mischievous. It was the first day of a new semester with a new history teacher; let's just call him Mr. Garris. Being new, he didn't know us from Adam. So Rex, Steve, and I decided to have a little fun. When, as teachers do, he called roll on that first day, we decided we would switch names. I was Rex, Steve was me, and Rex was Steve. Unbelievably, it worked perfectly. When Mr. Garris called our names we raised our hands, wrong names respectively, and said, "Here."

As often happens with teens, everyone else in the class was on our side; and though there were snickers, the new teacher fell for it. We continued this way for weeks. When the teacher called the name my folks had given me, David, students might look at me, but it was Steve who answered. When I raised my hand, the teacher called out "Rex," and assuming that identity, I responded accordingly.

We even made sure to call each other by the wrong names as we passed Mr. Garris in the hallway. We laughed; others did, too. Mr. Garris knew something was up. Bless his heart, he just didn't know what. For us, it was great fun.

That is, it was fun until about midterm when we were going to have our first big exam. The question was: Did we want others taking tests for us? Though we were good friends, we didn't trust each other enough to continue.

We decided to switch back to our real names, pronto. The week leading up to the exam, Mr. Garris would call "Rex," and the real Rex would answer, though the teacher was looking at me. Et cetera. It was great fun, everyone had lots of laughs, and, being good-natured and outnumbered, Mr. Garris went with the flow. (Yet for the rest of that school term, he threatened to get us mixed up when grades for report cards were turned in.)

It has been said that the sweetest word a person ever hears is his own name. Hearing your name called for an award or recognition is a kind of magical thing. Hearing your name called when the circumstances are less laudatory (say for a court case, sentencing, or punishment) has an equally powerful, though opposite, effect.

In our culture, there's that first name given to us by our parents, which may differ from the saint's name given at baptism, chrismation, tonsuring, or ordination. And then there's the surname, the last name, the one that carries more weight in the big picture than the first name.

I can still hear the women talking when I was a kid: "Oh, her? I hear she married a Robinson."

"Oh, really?"

Or: "Yes, it turns out it was one of those Lowder boys got into an argument with old man Simpson."

Or: "Her? Well, she used to be a Hatley, till she married one of the Whitleys. And you know how they are!"

Et cetera.

Southern men talk the same way, just with fewer words:

"Who?"

"Simpson."

"Ted's son?"

"Yep."

"Shot him?"

"Unh-huh."

"That Lowder boy—married that Hatley girl?"

"Whitley."

Anyway, you see it's that last name that carries a lot of responsibility; the first name, not as much.

I remember Bishop Basil telling of his grandmother's advice before he headed off to college. She told him to stay out of trouble (i.e., jail), not so much because of who he was—his first name—but *whose* he was: his last name. In other words, don't shame the family name.

In our culture, this family name is normally passed on through males. The woman takes the man's family name at the time of marriage. Though this tradition got a bit murky as we waded through the latter half of the last century, it's still the norm.

There was a time when certain women would boast, "Oh, I kept my maiden name."

To which an old friend would reply, "I see, instead of taking your husband's name, you kept your father's."

With that family name comes great responsibility. Due to the failures or successes of those who've gone before, we are each given an opportunity to carry on the family name, to continue it, redeem it, or, let's be honest, to tarnish it. By our actions *that* name is judged. It reflects, for good or ill, on the whole family.

Once, on a plane ride from Charlotte, North Carolina, to Houston, Texas, I sat beside a woman who was on a mission. She was tracing her family line, her ancestry, and was coming to Houston to interview an elderly aunt. Later, she and some family members were to fly to Ireland to continue this backward trek, filling in the names on their family tree. She was even kin to a Huneycutt. But she didn't have much information on Huneycutts other than the knowledge that the majority of them are pretty much all born and bred in my home county in North Carolina. (In other words, we Huneycutts don't get out much.)

As she shared stories she'd discovered of dead relatives, it only reinforced for me the brevity of our lives—how very little time we have to carry that family name, to further the cause, whatever the cause may be. It's not, as the grave markers reveal, just a birth date and a death date. Everyone will have those, no matter your character. It is what is done on the space of that little dash, between those two dates, that matters.

This lady had traveled to many graveyards tracing her family line. She also had a large folder full of pictures, old pictures, of dead relatives. One of the black-and-white photos was of a fellow with short pants, shirt unbuttoned, a cigar in his grinning mouth, with a hat on his head. I said, "He looks like a character." She said he was. I said, "They don't make characters any more." She said, "No, these days we only expect Hollywood stars to be characters."

Years ago, at the graduation banquet of St. Herman Seminary, Kodiak, Alaska, the outgoing dean, Fr. Chad Hatfield, reflected to the graduating class:

> When my sons were teenagers, I would often remind them, when they were going out the door to meet friends at some kind of gathering of other teenagers—"remember who I am!" I was confident that they knew full well who they were, but they needed to remember who I was. I am, of course, their father. But I am also "a Father," as a priest of the Church. They are, by virtue of being my sons, tied to my identity. We share the same family name. Their actions, for good or for ill, reflect back on me and their mother. The fact that I am a priest reflects back onto the Orthodox Christian Church. There is no denying or escaping this fact of life. Right or wrong, this is just how it is in this world of ours.

And this is true—true for all of us, not just priests and priests' kids. We all bear the same family name: Christian. Bought with a price, we are sons of God the Father through adoption in His Son. We are grafted into this family through new birth—being born again—in baptism.

That Blood that flows from that chalice, in the Eucharist, unites us as one *true* family. Thus, no matter our differences—cultural, ethnic, political, or social—we are kin to each other through that Blood, the Blood of Christ poured out for us on Calvary, manifest in the chalice of Holy Communion.

Oh, sure, we are all related through Adam. But that relationship leads only to death. Our kinship with the New Adam, Christ, leads to life eternal with the saints: our kin, our family (after all, we share the same Christian bloodline), who've gone on before us.

Thus, in a very real way, we are responsible not only for our own name, the one given us by Mom and Dad, and/or the one conferred on us by the Church. We are not only responsible for that name given us by our father or husband. We are responsible for the name Christian. For, as our Lord said, "For whoever is ashamed of Me and My words, of him the Son of Man will be ashamed when He comes in His own glory, and in His Father's, and of the holy angels" (Luke 9:26).

How do we sinners honor this great name of Christ? We honor it by remembering that name, Christ, before all others. In 2 Corinthians, St. Paul writes:

> For we do not preach ourselves, but Christ Jesus the Lord, and ourselves your bondservants for Jesus' sake. For it is the God who commanded light to shine out of darkness, who has shone in our hearts to give the light of the knowledge of the glory of God in the face of Jesus Christ. But we have this treasure in earthen vessels, that the excellence of the power may be of God and not of us. We are hard-pressed on every side, yet not crushed; we are perplexed, but not in despair; persecuted, but not forsaken; struck down, but not destroyed—always carrying about in the body the dying of the Lord Jesus, that the life of Jesus also may be manifested in our body. (2 Corinthians 4:5–10)

Brothers and sisters (I can call y'all that because, in Christ, we are family), if we wish that others would see Christ in us, we must first see Christ in them. That's just the way it works; to see it any other way only leads away from the Name that is above all names, Christ the Lord. In the end, it's not so much whether we know the name of Christ, but whether Christ knows our name according to our deeds of love done in His name.

"Let your light so shine before men, that they may see your good works and glorify your Father in heaven" (Matthew 5:16).

An Empty Church
Is a Peaceful Church

Here follows my special interview with Fr. Danislav
Gregorio, pastor of St. Swithin's by the Swamp in Appleton, Indiana.

JH: Welcome, Fr. Danislav!

DG: Thank you, Fr. Joseph, I am happy (so far) to be here.

JH: Fr. Danislav has written a new book entitled, *An Empty Church
Is a Peaceful Church*. What an interesting title! Tell us, Father,
before we get into the substance of the book, how did you come
up with the title?

DG: Have you ever been in an empty church, Father?

JH: Well, of course . . .

DG: Wasn't it peaceful?

JH: Well . . . yes, of course.

DG: Then you should understand why I titled my book, *An Empty
Church Is a Peaceful Church*.

JH: Okay, fine. I must inform our listeners that I have only read *half*
of the book, mainly because the other half is written in a foreign language. Why, Fr. Danislav, did you write only half the
book in English?

DG: Have you ever been to an Orthodox church service, Father?

JH: Huh! What a silly que—

DG: Well, then, you should understand why I wrote only half of the book in English!

JH: Yes, I see. Well, let's get into the book, shall we? In Chapter One you cover some matters of church etiquette wherein you mention that some people have been unhappy with your way of handling "rules and regs" and how to behave in church.

DG: You're referring, maybe, to that fellow who crossed his legs in church one Sunday during Matins?

JH: Yes, that'd be a good place to start. First, how big is your church?

DG: It holds around 500.

JH: And this was at Matins; how many do you normally have for Matins?

DG: Three, sometimes four—maybe as many as five.

JH: Okay, tell us about the leg-crossing guy.

DG: Well, he crossed his legs.

JH: Understood, Father; but how did you handle it?

DG: While censing the temple during the Ninth Ode, I simply went up to him and in a loud voice asked, "Are you comfortable? May I get you anything? A newspaper? A cup of coffee? Maybe a cigarette?"

JH: And this man ended up leaving your church?

DG: Indeed, he did. You see, he loved crossing his legs more than he loved obedience.

JH: But, Father—

DG: I did not come here to argue, Father. Please, stick to the book!

JH: All right, if you insist. Tell us about the itching powder on the icons. I mean, really—you put itching powder on the icons?

DG: I did indeed! Have you ever seen those icons after careless women reverence them with their lipstick? Disgusting!

JH: Agreed, but—

DG: Well! I solved that! You see, they kissed the icon only one time with the itching powder, and problem solved! Ho ho! You should have seen them!

JH: How'd that work out for you?

DG: They left the church, of course. I thought you said you'd read my book?

JH: I said I read only *half* your book. Anyway, we're talking today with the author of the new book, *An Empty Church Is a Peaceful Church,* Fr. Danislav Gregorio. Father, I must say, I was a bit shocked when I read that just after the words, "Blessed is the Kingdom . . ." you locked the doors of the church until the end of the service. Why?

DG: Do you see how many people come late to church? At my place— not any more!

JH: So . . .

DG: So nothing! It is rude to show up late to church!

JH: Well, I agree, but I have to ask: How did that affect your attendance?

DG: Father, the title of the book is *An Empty Church Is a Peaceful Church.* Believe me, these days my church is very peaceful.

JH: No doubt. No doubt. You said, Fr. Danislav, that there was a problem with some of the clothes the young ladies were wearing?

DG: No, I said there was a problem with the clothes they were *not* wearing! There were whole sections of their dresses that were— missing.

JH: And how did you handle that?

DG: I put it in my book.

JH: I know, Father, but you wrote that section in a foreign language!

DG: Oh. Yes, of course. Father, what do you call someone who speaks two languages?

JH: Bilingual.

DG: How about someone who speaks three languages?

JH: Trilingual.

DG: Ah. But what do you call someone who speaks only one language?

JH: Uh—?

DG: *American!* Ha! Me make joke. Seriously, in my country, back in the good ol' days, women wore modest clothing; these days, here in America, not so much.

JH: But if you wrote that section in a foreign language, how are they ever to benefit from your encouragement to do the right thing?

DG: The right thing? They did the right thing! They left the church! Ha ha!

JH: Oh, I see. You make joke?

DG: No. I am serious. In 1950s, in my country, this is how the church should be. Now *those* were the days!

JH: For those of you who may have just joined us—

DG: See, you are late! You should be ashamed! You should be on time!

JH: It's okay, Father, calm down; this is a radio interview. It's okay! My guest today is Fr. Danislav Gregorio, who has written a new book entitled, *An Empty Church Is a Peaceful Church*. Father, I am absolutely shocked—*shocked*—by what you have revealed today. Your attitude toward the souls that God has sent you . . .

DG: God? Huh! I sent them back to their god!

JH: Father, please let me finish. I find the most shocking part to be the section concerning what you did with their cell phones.

DG: Yes! Wasn't that wonderful?

JH: Wonderful? Father, I'm not sure what you did is legal!

DG: Legal? Ha! Cell phones, cell phones . . . always ringing, ringing . . . disco ring tones, birds chirping, hip hop! I've had it! *Had it,* I tell you!

JH: Father, may I please borrow your cell phone a sec?

DG: Wha—?

JH: Just give it to me.

DG: Oka-a-a-y . . .

BOMP!
CRASH!
(I knocked him out with his cell phone.)
Whew. Okay. I'm sorry, y'all. I just couldn't take it anymore. He's out cold. Forgive me while I address him. I know he'll listen later to a recording of this radio interview.

Father! The church has always had squabbles and issues, struggles and complications—even from the time of St. Paul. In Galatians we read:

> Brethren, if a man is overtaken in any trespass, you who are spiritual restore such a one in a spirit of gentleness, considering yourself lest you also be tempted. Bear one another's burdens, and so fulfill the law of Christ. For if anyone thinks himself to be something, when he is nothing, he deceives himself. (Galatians 6:1–3)

Then in Romans 12:

> Let love be without hypocrisy. Abhor what is evil. Cling to what is good. Be kindly affectionate to one another with brotherly love, in honor giving preference to one another; not lagging in diligence, fervent in spirit, serving the Lord; rejoicing in hope, patient in tribulation, continuing steadfastly in prayer; distributing to the needs of the saints, given to hospitality. Bless those who persecute you; bless and do not curse. Rejoice with those who rejoice, and weep with those who weep. Be of the same mind toward one another. Do not set your mind on high things, but associate with the humble. Do not be wise in your own opinion. Repay no one evil for evil. Have regard for good things in the sight of all men. If it is possible, as much as depends on you, live peaceably with all men. (Romans 12:9–18)

And also in Romans 15:

> We then who are strong ought to bear with the scruples of the weak, and not to please ourselves. Let each of us please his neighbor for his good, leading to edification. For even Christ did not please Himself; but as it is written, "The

reproaches of those who reproached You fell on Me." For whatever things were written before were written for our learning, that we through the patience and comfort of the Scriptures might have hope. Now may the God of patience and comfort grant you to be like-minded toward one another, according to Christ Jesus, that you may with one mind and one mouth glorify the God and Father of our Lord Jesus Christ. Therefore receive one another, just as Christ also received us, to the glory of God. (Romans 15:1–7)

Father Danislav, the writings of St. Paul—heck, most of the New Testament—are about love and mercy, bearing one another's burdens, *especially* sinners. Don't forget to read your Bible! Regarding struggle and strife within the parish, I'll tell you a little story:

In one parish there was a disagreement about whether to do bows from the waist or full prostrations during the services of the Great Fast (Lent). Some said that during the holy season, at the appointed times, all present must make a full prostration (kneeling, face to the ground). Others were just as adamant about bows from the waist being the traditional way. The situation intensified to the point that parishioners were not only yelling at each other, but almost coming to blows.

Finally, someone suggested that they go visit the hermit, Elder Sosimas, who lived in the forest. His age, experience, and wisdom would surely guide them to the ancient way of the Church. So off they went to see the elder.

When they found him, both sides related, with great emotion, their respective positions: some said bows, others said prostrations. Getting carried away in their zeal, and almost coming to blows in front of the elder, they ceased fighting long enough to ask, "Holy Father, as you see, during this holy season of Lent, we have almost come to blows, our parish is being rent at the seams, we are at war with each other. Tell us, what is the ancient way of the Church?"

The elder looked at them with tears streaming down his face, his heart aching, and said, "But, my dear children, this is the ancient way of the Church!"

Heh! The more things change, the more they remain the same. The Good News is: God never changes. Christ is the same yesterday, today, and forever. And when seeking peace in our churches, it must be His peace, the peace that passes all understanding, which we seek.

Otherwise, as Fr. Danislav, my poor mistaken guest, has stated, it is only an empty church that is a peaceful one.

A Funny Thing Happened on the Way to Phronema

A priest friend of mine who used to serve as a cop in New York City tells of Mother Teresa's visit to the Big Apple. He'd always admired Mother Teresa's work among the destitute in India and hoped he would be able to meet her. Sure enough, he was given VIP guard duty for her visit, and one day, amid the whirlwind of her tour, he was finally able to ask her the question that had been burning in his mind. The cop leaned down to Mother Teresa and asked, "Mother Teresa, I've always wanted to know: how do you do it? I mean, what is it that really keeps you going?"

He saw a twinkle appear in her eyes and she slowly began to smile. She motioned for him to lean closer. He was beyond excited. *The* Mother Teresa of Calcutta was going to answer his question, "What keeps you going?" As he leaned his ear lower, he heard this saintly woman say, "Frequent flier miles!"

The Sunday after Pentecost is the Sunday of All Saints. Have you ever read the lives of the saints? Depressing, huh? It can be overwhelming to read the stories of venerable men and women who seemed so courageous, unmovable, holy and, well, kinda perfect.

Then there's the most common saint story. It's short, so listen carefully. It goes something like this: The Turks, Mohammedans, Romans, somebody is persecuting the Christians, and suddenly, someone in the crowd cries out, "I, too, am a Christian!" *Slash. Bomp. Ka-thud.* The end.

The stories of saints can be violent. But what courage! What zeal! What . . . *what* . . . what can I possibly do to compare?

The answer is: Be faithful. That's all we're called to do. Be faithful. Many people around us live God-pleasing lives, saintly lives, worthy of emulation—primarily due to their faithfulness. Amid the cares and bustle of life, their example might go unnoticed. In fact, their humble fumbles may actually serve as a temptation.

Take, for instance, Subdeacon Andrew. Subdeacon Andrew was a joy. He'd served for over forty years as a deacon in the Episcopal Church before converting to Orthodoxy back in 1996. By the time he was ordained a subdeacon, he was nearly eighty years old. This, coupled with his childlike nature, no guile at all, made for some delightfully erroneous moments in the altar.

Once, while I was outside the Holy Doors preparing to chant a litany, the subdeacon came out of the north side angel door and stood by me. Thinking he was going to ask me a question or tell me something when the litany was over, I paid him no mind.

The Psalms being ended by the chanters, I commenced the great litany of Matins. After about four petitions I looked over at him, still standing by my side, and raised my eyebrow. He smiled and went back to happily staring at the icons on the iconostasis.

While the chanters replied to one of the petitions, I leaned over and said, "What are you doing here?"

He turned, draped his arms around my neck, hugged me, and said with a big smile, "I don't know!" He laughed. We laughed. He retired to the altar.

One Sunday, I'd gotten up early and realized we had no bread for oblation. My long-suffering wife arose and made the bread just in time for Matins. While I was puttering around making sure all the preparations for Liturgy were in order, I noticed the subdeacon cutting up the holy bread, the antidoron, for distribution to the faithful. Yet about every fifth piece was being popped into his mouth!

"Are you going to receive Communion today?" I asked.

"Plannin' to," he mumbled, mid-chew.

"Then stop eating up all the holy bread!"

He honestly had not realized what he was doing. He looked a bit embarrassed and said, "Oh, my gosh! I'm so sorry. But it smells so good!"

My favorite story happened one night following Vespers. We had a new family in the church whose beloved mother/grandmother had died the year before. The daughter, a grown woman with grandchildren of her own, wanted us to serve a pannikhida (memorial service). The whole family was gathered, and the family matriarch was crying as the choir began. Subdeacon Andrew came out and stood by me, beside the memorial table. When it was about time for the censer, I went to receive it from him, but he was empty-handed.

I said, "Go get me the censer."

Into the altar he went. The choir was singing beautifully. He soon exited the altar and handed me the censer. I went to bless the incense. There wasn't even charcoal inside.

Meanwhile the matriarch's crying, the choir is singing . . .

I whispered, "There's no charcoal." Back into the altar went the subdeacon. He quickly returned, handing me the censer.

You guessed it. There was charcoal, but no incense! It dawned on him about this time that I was trembling. Back he went.

Meanwhile the matriarch's crying, the choir is singing . . .

Quickly the aged and beloved subdeacon reappeared with a censer and lighted charcoal. But, alas, the incense had fallen off the target and wasn't smoking.

Here's where I took charge. Sometimes it's possible to tap the base of the censer on the floor, causing the incense to pop up onto, at least closer to, the charcoal. This I did. At precisely the moment of impact, one of the chains on the censer broke, and the contents of the censer (that would be, most importantly, a burning coal) spilled out onto the carpet.

Meanwhile the matriarch's crying, the choir is singing . . .

Book in one hand, broken censer in the other, I looked toward the subdeacon, in split seconds now become eternity; he resembled a major league umpire with hands on knees, staring down at the smoldering scene as if to see just what would become of it.

I stage-whispered, "Pick it up!"

(Now, really, who wants to pick up a burning piece of charcoal?) By the time he said, "Wha—," I'd picked it up, burned my fingers, and put it in the censer. I grabbed the broken section of chain and did my best to cense the table in the normal fashion. All in all, I don't think the grieving family ever noticed. However, when it was all sung and done, I was beside myself.

We had an old friend staying with us as a house guest. By the time I made it next door to the rectory, I was slightly disturbed. I flung myself down into a chair and whined, "Is this my last day on earth?!"

To which he replied, "No—that was yesterday!"

Heh!

Phronema is a Greek term that is used in Eastern Orthodox theology to refer to mindset or outlook; it is the Orthodox mind. The attaining of phronema is a matter of practicing the correct faith (*orthodoxia*) in the correct manner (*orthopraxis*). Attaining phronema is regarded as the first step toward theosis, the state of glorification.

The good subdeacon, though full of late-life foibles, never said a word—a bad word—about anyone. *Anyone!* Never a bad word did he say about those who disliked him, slandered him, and mocked him—not one word. He refused to speak ill of his neighbor. *This* is an example of phronema.

St. Makarios of Egypt writes:

In accordance with divine providence, the devil was not sent at once to the Gehenna assigned to him, but his sentence was postponed in order to let him test and try man's free will. In this way, he unintentionally fosters greater maturity and righteousness in the saints by promoting their patient endurance, and so is the cause of their greater glory; and, at the same time, through his malevolence and his scheming against the saints he justifies more fully his own punishment.

All this is to say: *The struggle is good.*

The Sunday after Pentecost is a day set aside by the Church to remember all the saints. The very next day, Monday after All Saints Sunday, begins the summer fast in honor of the apostles. Let us ponder the lives of these men, men with clay feet, brothers who quarreled, men in need of repentance: Peter & Paul, great saints of the Church. Let us be mindful of our own need for phronema, for salvation, during the time of fasting. Persevere! All we are called to do is *be faithful.*

St. Maximos the Confessor writes:

Many of the things that befall us, befall us for our training, either to do away with past sins or to correct present neglect or to check future sinful deeds. He then, who reckons that temptation has come upon him for one of these reasons, is not vexed at its attack, especially as he is conscious of his sin.

Wouldn't it be nice if we got out of bed knowing full well that the Lord would send us trials to help us toward patience? If we got into our cars fully expecting the other drivers on the road to break all the rules, to help us toward patience? What if we determined, before our day even began, to look the other way when tempted by lust—and then followed through with our promise as soon, and often, as possible? What if we decided, just for one day, to go without participating in gossip, anger, swearing, or gluttony? (What if you are already doing this and I am the only one missing the boat?)

Part V

Saints, Singers, and Superheroes

Constantine: He Built the City, But He Didn't Write the Song!

A friend of mine is a priest in a big Greek church named after mother and son saints, Helen and Constantine. When I say this is a big Greek church, I don't mean just a big temple, parking lot, annual festival, and gymnasium; of course they have all that! I mean they've got something special, way down in the basement. I never would have believed it, had I not seen it with my own eyes.

Y'all, they have a time machine! That's right, an honest-to-goodness time machine that will transport you to any destination you wish. Well, almost. That is, you can go anywhere within the so-called "Christian Era"—and your destination has to be connected with a saint. Being one for new adventures, I said, "Sure, I'm game! How 'bout we try the Great Emperor Constantine?"

So I pulled the lever and *whoosh*! I was really taken aback, being hurled through the ages at lightning speed: head swimming and colossal noises. Next thing I knew I was hurled down into a ramshackle house, a bit of a hovel, and people kept calling me "Bernie." (For some reason, "Bernie" appears to be my time travel name.)

Anyway, there came a loud knock at the door, and I opened it to see three frazzled and haggard hippie types come rushing into my house, saying, "Bernie! You're not going to believe what happened!"

I said, "Where am I?"

They looked at me curiously and said, "Bernie, you're in Rome, it's the year 313, and you're always babbling about that silly thing you call a time machine. Now sit down and listen!"

I didn't know what else to do but sit down. Then they related their tale of woe: "Bernie, it was Saturday and we were worshipping in the community worship center, you know: wearing jeans, banging tambourines, strumming our guitars and singing the ancient hymn—"

I said, "Kumbaya?"

"No! You know: 'Our God is an awesome God.' Anyway, on about the eighteenth time through the chorus, word came down that Emperor Constantine had ruined the Church!"

"What?" I asked. "You mean he demanded PowerPoint® presentations and use of the words *emergent* and *post-modern*?"

"No, silly," they replied. "He wants us to do church on Sunday, pray to the dead, worship Mary, wear gold vestments, and call ourselves Catholics! And this from a man who worships the S-U-N!"

It was at that point that I absentmindedly pulled back on the handle at my side, thinking it was a recliner, and *poof!* I was off traveling again. Whirling, whirling . . .

This time, thanks to the time machine, I found myself plopped down and facing none other than Alex Trebek! I was on the set of *Jeopardy*, and Alex was saying, "Bernie, you're in the lead."

I said, "Bad Songs of the '70s for 600, please."

Alex: "This pop protest song went to number one in the UK, sung by a group called Paper Lace. It was made popular in the States by Bo Donaldson and the Heywoods. Take a listen:

"Billy, don't be a hero! Don't be a fool with your life!
Billy, don't be a hero! Come back and make me your wife!

"For 600, name the writer of this song."

The gal to my left, Tamara (I believe her name was), hit the buzzer first and said, "Who is Constantine?"

"Gee!" I thought, "Constantine's getting the blame for everything bad!" Of course, that was the wrong answer. As I hit my button, you guessed it, I was transported through time to another location. Much to my astonishment, I wound up inside of a novel. It soon became clear to me where I was: I was inside Dan Brown's *Da Vinci Code*.

Someone was saying, "At this gathering [Council of Nicea, 325], many aspects of Christianity were debated and voted upon—the date of Easter, the role of the bishops, the administration of sacraments . . ."

"Okay," I thought, "so far so good."

". . . and, of course, the *divinity* of Jesus."

Whoa! What?

The character went on, "Until *that* moment in history, Jesus was viewed by His followers as a mortal prophet—a great and powerful man, but a man nonetheless. A mortal . . . Jesus' establishment as 'the Son of God' was officially proposed and voted on by the Council of Nicea."

Y'all? *Total. Utter. Can you hear me? Nonsense.*

In reality, early Christians overwhelmingly worshipped Jesus Christ as their risen Savior and Lord. Before the creeds, early Christian leaders developed a "rule" or "canon" of faith, which affirmed this truth. To take one example, the canon of prominent second-century bishop Irenaeus took its cue from 1 Corinthians 8:6: "Yet for us there is but one God, the Father, from whom all things came and for whom we live; and there is but one Lord, Jesus Christ."

And the Council of Nicea? It was the first ecumenical council of the Church, made possible by the patronage of Constantine and his desire to end the disunity and controversy being caused by the Arian heresy.

Here's the back story:

The Alexandrian priest, Arius, was known for his preaching and asceticism. Yet, around the year 319, he gained attention for teaching that Jesus was not fully divine, but was less than the Father—a creature—a lesser god.

An Alexandrian synod condemned this teaching a year later, but Arius's teachings still gained in popularity—in part, due to his creation of catchy songs (kind of like "Billy Don't Be a Hero") proclaiming doctrinal beliefs. Constantine, hoping to quell a theological rebellion in his empire, called together all the bishops in hopes of ending the controversy.

On May 20, 325, over three hundred bishops, most of them from the East, convened at Nicea (north of Constantinople). The council ended two months later on July 25. Many of those who attended the council were simple Greek-speaking pastors who had earned the title of "confessor" by having endured imprisonment and punishment for the sake of their faith. Thus, they weren't impressed by Arius's innovations.

Anyway, the moron in Brown's book went on to say, "Constantine commissioned and financed a new Bible, which omitted those gospels that spoke of Christ's human traits and embellished those gospels that made Him godlike. The earlier gospels were outlawed, gathered up, and burned."

Mon Dieu! 'Tis garbahge! Constantine wouldn't know a new Bible if it bit him in the back. It wasn't on the council's agenda. Besides, the earliest source of New Testament writings is from St. Paul, shortly after the Ascension, during the apostolic age. Someone should have clued Brown in, or else Constantine and cohorts should have taken St. Paul's writings out. But, of course, Brown's no dummy. My guess is he presumed we are.

You know, it was at this point, having traveled in the time machine back to the year 313, then to the TV game show, *Jeopardy*, and from there to the fictional *Da Vinci Code* book, that I had a thought: I could cut out the parts of Dan Brown's novel that were heretical and help to save the day!

So, I reached down for what I'd thought was my sword and pulled it, only to realize that it was the lever of the time machine, which brought me back, thank goodness, to the present moment.

Whew. I told my friend who showed me the machine all that I had seen in regard to Constantine, and he related to me these facts:

Constantine was born in what is now known as Serbia around

the year 280. He was the only son of Helen, whose former husband, Constantius, was later elevated to Caesar. Upon his father's death in 306, Constantine was proclaimed ruler by the troops. The history gets a little messy here—but, fast-forwarding a bit, we find Constantine on the eve of a battle receiving a vision. A cross of light appeared in front of the sun, and he heard a voice, saying, "In this sign conquer."

Profoundly affected by this revelation, Constantine had a large cross made to be borne into battle, himself wearing the sign of the cross, and his charges bearing the emblem on their shields. After his victory, to show his gratitude to the God of the Christians, Constantine granted religious liberty, thereby "legalizing" Christian worship, in his famous Edict of Milan of 313. It wasn't until 325, following another victory, that the Roman Empire was united under a sole ruler, Constantine. Shortly thereafter, he moved the capital of the empire from Rome to "New Rome," or Constantinople.

Though his "conversion experience" happened with the vision of the heavenly cross, Constantine was also influenced by his moral conscience, military leaders, and government rulers who had embraced the Faith. This sudden turn of events—religious liberty, the end of the persecutions, and the freeing of Christian prisoners—brought about a joyous time that most Christians had thought impossible. One ancient writer, Tertullian, had previously written, "But the Caesars also would have believed in Christ, if either the Caesars had not been necessary to the world or if Christians too could have been Caesars." Constantine's reign proved otherwise. For the rest of his life, Constantine's efforts were toward *uniting* the empire and the Church.

While it is true that Constantine attempted to hold his empire together politically by showing equal favor to Christianity and the practice of sun worship, to claim that he continued to worship the sun after his "conversion" is historically false. Time would prove that mixing the major religions in a form of syncretism was not the answer. Under his administration, magic and divination were suppressed. As for the age-old practice of emperor worship, though many practices continued, Constantine abolished the practice of sacrifice to the emperor. And, much as the earlier Peace of Rome (*Pax Romana*) is historically hailed as aiding the spread of the Gospel, Constantine's allowing bishops to use the imperial mail service did much to spread Christ's Church.

No new doctrine was invented by the Council of Nicea or by Constantine himself. Contrary to popular lore (e.g., Dan Brown's bestseller, *The Da Vinci Code*), the Bible's contents were not ratified at the Nicene Council, Jesus was not "elected" Son of God, Mary Magdalene was not part of the agenda, and various other gospels were not suppressed. Rather, the bishops upheld what they maintained had always been the understanding of the universal Church of Christ: the Son is co-equal, co-eternal, "one in essence" with the Father.

With the ascension of Constantine to supreme ruler, the first period of the Christian era (apostles, Pentecost, and persecutions) came to a close. Where at one time the Roman authorities had tried to snuff out the Christian faith, the tables turned, and it was now time for pagans to go underground. In 330, after his inauguration, Constantine proclaimed that pagan services would no longer be performed within Constantinople. Under his reign, Constantine showed many favors to the Christian Church, and the law of the land reflected Christian principles. Along with being a great benefactor of the Church, in 321 he ordered that the day of Christian worship, Sunday, be made a public holiday.

I mean, don't get me wrong—Constantine was not without faults. His sins and shortcomings were many, including the killing of his son and his second wife due to rumors and confusion about an illicit affair between them. Yet there is no denying his historical importance and pivotal role in the flourishing of the Christian Church.

Constantine had hoped to be baptized in the Jordan, but ill health prevented it. Instead, shortly after Easter in 337,

Constantine was baptized in the suburbs of Nicomedia by, ironically, the Arian bishop Eusebius. (It should be noted that postponing baptism until late in life, near death, was a common practice in the fourth century.) Constantine died not long after, on the Feast of Pentecost, May 22. His body was interred in Constantinople, in the Church of the Twelve Apostles. Constantine is honored, along with his mother, Helen, as a saint in the Orthodox Church—feast day, May 21.

All right, all right, it's time for me to 'fess up about the time machine. I told a story. There ain't no such thing. But it's about as factual as a lot of other things folks outside the Church try to pin on Constantine.

And besides, so what if he *had* written "Billy Don't Be a Hero"? That's not nearly as bad as "All by Myself" by Eric Carmen, "Feelings" by Morris Albert, "Tragedy" by the Bee Gees, or "We Built This City" by Starship; so enough about Constantine.

But speaking of bad songs, and kind of related to Constantine, is Helen—Helen Reddy, that is; you know: "I Am Woman (Hear Me Roar)"? That song earned her a Grammy Award for Female Pop Vocal Performance in 1973. At the awards ceremony, Helen Reddy concluded her acceptance speech by famously thanking God "because *She* makes everything possible."

So you see, friends, it just goes to show ya: bad songs, bad novels, and bad theology can often give good folks bad names.

People for the Ethical Treatment of . . . Dragons?

Thursday, July 26, started out like any other day. That is, until 10:30 A.M.

I live and work in Houston, Texas. My parish is St. George. And it is on that day, Thursday, July 26, that I must begin this old-style detective tale.

As I said, it was like any other day, except for the big black SUV that pulled into St. George Church parking lot at approximately 10:30 A.M. From my office window, I only noticed that I did not recognize the man emerging in the dark Ray-Ban sunglasses. That's nothing unusual; it's a big parish in a big city. And sunglasses in Houston are as common as acne in junior high.

Things got a little more curious when the secretary, Diane, yelled back to me, "Fr. Joseph, a Mr. Mister here to see you."

Having survived the eighties, I'd heard of Mr. Mister; they were a popular band who'd had a couple of hit songs back in the day. The chorus of their hit, "Broken Wings," was later sampled on the 2Pac single "Until the End of Time." They had several number one MTV videos and headlined the first MTV Spring Break show in 1986. Mr. Mister had several Grammy Award nominations, including the 1986 Grammy for "Best Pop Band" (which was awarded to the "We Are the World" ensemble).

During this time, Mr. Mister toured with other popular acts including Don Henley, the Bangles, Eurythmics, Adam Ant, and Tina Turner. They even had a song called "Kyrie" that began with the words "Kyrie Eleison." (It was probably my first exposure to Greek Orthodoxy, though I had no idea.) But I digress.

I yelled, "Who?"

"A Mr. Mister," she said.

Oh well, though I'd thought they were a band—a group of guys—stranger things have happened. So I walked out into the foyer and greeted Mr. Mister: "Hello, I'm Fr. Joseph."

"Mr. Mister," he replied. "I represent People for the Ethical Treatment of Dragons. You got a place where we can sit down?"

"Sure," I said, and led him toward my office.

After all the niceties and comments about the weather—which in Houston often goes something like this: "Gee, it sure is hot!" or, "Wow, is it ever hot!" yet sometimes it goes like this: "Rain? Rain. Dang! That's *some rain!*"—Mr. Mister said, "My organization, People for the Ethical Treatment of Dragons, is not very pleased with your church."

"Sir, er, I mean, Mister," I stammered, "uh, Mr. Mister: what, exactly, are you talking about?"

He said, "What I'm talking about, Fr. Joseph, is the mosaic above your church door depicting a man on a horse brutalizing a poor helpless dragon. It is just such mean-spirited depictions that, throughout history, have painted dragons in a bad light."

"St. George is one of the most beloved saints in the world," I replied. "He lived in the late third century—"

"But," Mr. Mister cried, "he was cruel to dragons!"

"Well, that may be," I said, "but a very cruel emperor named Diocletian was in charge of the Roman Empire. He hated Christians. St. George was a Christian warrior and a very brave fighter. He served in the army of Rome as an officer. He loved Christ. After many years, he finally stopped serving the army because he would not worship the pagan gods."

Mr. Mister chimed in, "I believe you are mistaken. I happen to know that St. George was from England."

"Many people say St. George was from England," I replied, "but this is only a legend. St. George was really a Syrian. He was tortured and died for Christ in Nikomedia, a town in Asia Minor, in AD 303. The courage of St. George helped many people become Christians. The icon of St. George on his horse killing the dragon shows us the fight between good and evil. St. George represents the Sons of Light and the dragon represents the Dragon of Darkness. The first church to have St. George's name was built by Emperor Constantine the Great in the Holy Land. Afterwards many churches carried the name St. George. He is one of the greatest martyrs for Christ. We remember St. George the Great Martyr on April 23."

Mr. Mister shouted, "But, Fr. Joseph, what about the dragon?"

"What about the dragon?" I said. "Listen, Diocletian's second in command was Galerius, the conqueror of Persia and an avid supporter of the pagan religion. As a result of a rumor that the Christians were plotting the death of Galerius, an edict was issued that all Christian churches were to be destroyed and all Scriptures to be burnt. Anyone admitting to being a Christian would lose his rights as a citizen, if not his life.

"As a consequence, Diocletian took strict action against any alternative forms of religion in general and the Christian faith in particular. He achieved the reputation of being perhaps the cruelest persecutor of Christians at that time.

"Many Christians feared to be loyal to their God; but, having become a convert to Christianity, St. George acted to limit the excesses of Diocletian's actions against the Christians. He went to the city of Nicomedia, where, upon entering, he tore down the notice of the emperor's edict. St. George gained great respect for his compassion towards Diocletian's victims.

"As news spread of his rebellion against the persecutions, St. George realized that, as both Diocletian and Galerius were in the city, it would not be long before he was arrested. He prepared for the event by disposing of his property to the poor and freeing his slaves.

"When he appeared before Diocletian, it is said that St. George bravely denounced him for his unnecessary cruelty and injustice and that he made an eloquent and courageous speech. He stirred the populace with his powerful and convincing rhetoric against the imperial decree to persecute Christians. Diocletian refused to acknowledge or accede to St. George's reasoned, reproachful condemnation of his actions. The emperor consigned St. George to prison with instructions that he be tortured until he denied his faith in Christ. St. George, having defended his faith, was beheaded at Nicomedia in Palestine on the twenty-third of April in the year AD 303."

"Yes, well, thank you for the History Channel plug, Fr. Joseph," snarled Mr. Mister. "But you've yet to explain the massacre of the dragon that is depicted on that horrible mosaic outside your church!"

"What can I say?" I said. "The legends about St. George spread far and wide, and it was claimed that in a Libyan town a dragon dwelt, keeping the population in terror. To satiate him the population tethered animal after animal, until they had no more. They then provided human sacrifices, and in ultimate desperation, a young princess was selected, named Cleolinda. The story then relates how St. George rode up on his white charger, dismounted, and fought the monster on foot, until it eventually succumbed. He then dragged the dying monster into the city, using the girdle of the princess, and slew the dragon in front of the people. St. George was greeted as their savior, and the king offered him a bag of gold as a reward for saving his daughter. This he refused and asked that it be given to the poor.

"The story is a powerful allegory, emblematic of the triumph of good over evil; but it also teaches of extreme endurance in the Christian faith and the trust that at all times should be placed in the Almighty by the invocation of the name of St. George, soldier, saint, and martyr."

"I think you're crazy," said Mr. Mister, "just plain crazy!"

"Why, thank you," I said. "That brings me to my conclusion—"

"The dragon!" he screamed.

"Be patient," I replied. "There is a tradition in the Holy Land of Christians and Muslims going to an Eastern Orthodox shrine for St. George at Beit Jala. This was attested to in 1866 by Elizabeth Finn, who wrote, 'St. George killed the dragon in this country [Palestine]; and the place is shown close to Beyroot [*sic*]. Many churches and convents are named after him. The church at Lydda is dedicated to St. George: so is a convent near Bethlehem, and another small one just opposite the Jaffa gate; and others beside. The Arabs believe that St. George can restore mad people to their senses; and to say a person has been sent to St. George's is equivalent to saying he has been sent to a madhouse. It is singular that the Moslem Arabs, as well as the Christians, share this veneration for St. George and send their mad people to be cured by him.'

"William Dalrymple visited the place in 1995. He wrote, 'I asked around in the Christian Quarter in Jerusalem, and discovered that the place was very much alive. With all the greatest shrines in the Christian world to choose from, it seemed that when the local Arab Christians had a problem—an illness, or something more complicated: a husband detained in an Israeli prison camp, for example—they preferred to seek the intercession of St. George in his grubby little shrine at Beit Jala rather than praying at the Holy Sepulchre in Jerusalem or the Church of the Nativity in Bethlehem.' He asked the priest at the shrine, 'Do you get many Muslims coming here?' The priest replied, 'We get hundreds! Almost as many as the Christian pilgrims. Often, when I come in here, I find Muslims all over the floor, in the aisles, up and down.'

"So you see, Mr. Mister," I concluded, "for you to call me crazy—here in this parish named for St. George—is fitting. Many, *many* people who are *crazy* seek the intercessions of St. George. Now what was it that brought you here?"

"The dragon," he said.

"Ah yes, the dragon," I replied. "If you're asking me whether, 1700 years ago, St. George speared a reptile, I cannot say. But anyone whose prayers have been answered through the intercession of the Great Martyr George *knows* the answer to that question. For as St. Paul says: 'For the message of the cross is foolishness to those who are perishing, but to us who are being saved it is the power of God' (1 Corinthians 1:18). 'For since, in the wisdom of God, the world through wisdom did not know God, it pleased God through the foolishness of the message preached to save those who believe' (1 Corinthians 1:21).

"By the way," I continued, "The group Mr. Mister had a big hit back in the eighties and the lyrics were a little confusing. Was it, 'Carry a laser down this road that I must travel,' or, 'Kill me a lizard on the road that I must follow'?"

"Look, I get this all the time," my visitor replied. "I was not part of the eighties music scene or the group Mr. Mister. My real name is George. In fact, my parents were very devoted. My name is George George, hence people call me Mr. Mister."

"Wait. Your parents were Arabs?" I asked.

"No," he said, "they were English *and* crazy. But I do know the answer to your question. The correct lyrics to the Mr. Mister song are: '*Kyrie eleison* down the road that I must travel.'"

"Hummph," I thought, "*Kyrie eleison* down the road that I must travel." And with that, he was gone. Strange; I kinda liked, "Kill me a lizard on the road that I must follow."

St. George, Great Martyr and Trophy Bearer—pray for all us crazy people!

Saint **Elvis?**

....

Back in August of 1977, following the rigors of after-school football practice, I was leaving the practice field with my buddies when I noticed my mom and dad sitting in our 1966 Ford pickup truck; my mom was crying and my dad looked sad. I knew something, some tragedy, had happened.

As my mind raced to think of what friend or relative it might be, my mom stopped the sobs long enough to look my way through bloodshot eyes and blurt out, "Elvis is dead. Elvis died today, son."

Then she resumed crying. They were listening to the news on the radio. As I scanned the other cars in the high school parking lot, the mood could only be described as somber; all ears were tuned to their radios and news of the singer's death: Elvis.

My family was on a first-name basis with Elvis, as were most Southern working folks—with the King, the King of Rock-n-Roll. Truth be known, he'd seen us. That's right, ladies and gentlemen, back in 1972 we saw an Elvis Presley concert at the Charlotte Coliseum, and if you believe my mom's gal pal Pam, Elvis saw us! This was back before, as they often say, "he got fat." I was eleven or twelve and don't remember too much about the show, except that we sat behind the stage, and every time he would look back that way my mom's friend Pam would scream, "He looked right at me! Oh my gosh! Did you see that?! He looked right at me!"

It was about an hour's drive home from the coliseum, and Pam sat in total awestruck silence. But every now and then, she would snap out of her stupor long enough to scream, "Did you see him? He looked *right at* me!"

Yes, I grew up on Elvis. We saw every single Elvis movie, my mom and I. She had tons of his records and, if you promise not to laugh, lemme tell ya: We've even got a huge velvet painting of Elvis that she and my dad picked up on a trip to Mexico.

A while back, under a scorching sun at Graceland, his beloved home, fans streamed by Elvis Presley's grave for the thirtieth anniversary of his death. They came with their fond memories: "I can't describe how I feel about him because I've loved him since I was a teenager," said Katie Brown of Crittenden, Kentucky. "When I would hear him sing, I'd go into like a trance and nothing else around me mattered."

Pat Hillebrand of DuBois, Pennsylvania, said her graveside visit with friend Sandy Bartoletti of Saratoga Springs, New York, brought back memories of the Elvis concert they attended together in 1957 as fifteen-year-old schoolmates.

"We rubbed our hands on the stage and I didn't wash my hands for a week," Hillebrand said. "I had gum that I chewed in the air where he breathed and I kept it for like fifteen years."

Folks, I'm sure, there're probably some readers right now thinking, "What in the world does this have to do with anything?"

Well, don't blame me; I owe the following facts to the webpage of a Roman Catholic priest in England, Fr. Nicholas Schofield: Did you know that one of Elvis's early performances (1955) was at the Catholic Club in Helena, Arkansas? However, his unorthodox performance did not impress the parish priest, Fr. Keller, especially when the singer autographed a female fan's leg. "You are a disgrace to manhood," he was allegedly told. "Don't come back anymore."

Did you know that one of the leading ladies in two of Elvis's films is now a Roman Catholic nun? That's right; Dolores Hart starred alongside Elvis in *Loving You* (1957) and *King Creole* (1958). She left Hollywood in 1963 to become a Benedictine nun at the Abbey of Regina Laudis, Bethlehem, Connecticut, where she eventually became prioress. And, back in 1971, Elvis actually recorded a song, *a prayer*, to the Virgin Mary entitled, "The Miracle of the Rosary":

O Blessed Mother we pray to thee
Thanks for the miracle of your rosary
Only you can hold back Your holy Son's hand
Long enough for the whole world to understand
Hail, Mary full of grace
The Lord is with thee
Blessed art thou among women
And blessed is the fruit of thy womb, Jesus
O Holy Mary dear mother of God
Please pray for us sinners
Now and at the hour of our death
And we give thanks once again
For the miracle of your rosary.

True, it's not exactly Orthodox, but I'm getting to that part. To do that, we have to go back not to the 1970s, '60s, or '50s—not even to when Presley was born in 1935. Rather we have to travel back in time one thousand five hundred years to around the year 500. That was around the time of the baptism of the great saint of Wales: David.

St. David of Wales was known for his preaching and for founding monasteries and churches in Wales, Cornwall, and Brittany during an era of prevailing paganism. As bishop, David of Wales oversaw two synods and made pilgrimages to Jerusalem. St. David's Cathedral sits atop the site of a monastery he founded in the valley of Glyn Rhosyn in Pembrokeshire.

St. David's monastic rule required the brethren to pull the plough without benefit of animals. They subsisted on water, bread, salt, and herbs. Evenings were spent in prayer, reading, and writing. This simple life of severe asceticism proscribed owning personal possessions, eating meat, and drinking beer.

Once, when David of Wales was preaching in the middle of a crowd, folks in the back complained they could not see or hear him. Then, it is said, the very ground on which he was standing rose to form a small hill so that he could be seen and heard by all. Also, a dove alighted on the saint's shoulder as a sign of God's blessing.

So what does this have to do with Elvis? Okay, here's the deal: David of Wales was baptized by—are you ready for this?—*Saint Elvis*. That's right, there was a saint named Elvis, who was a bishop of the Irish See of Munster—thus, it would appear that Elvis is a legitimate baptismal name. (However, by way of footnote, I have to tell you that I once heard a bishop, during a talk in Nashville, Tennessee, discourage any priest from taking the name Elvis at ordination—for obvious reasons!)

And Elvis is also a Celtic name. In fact, rumors of his Celtic ancestry are familiar to Elvis aficionados. The King's ancestral seat has been variously placed in Paisley; the Preseli hills in west Wales; Ireland, where St. Elvis was bishop of Munster; and a Scottish village called Alves, which residents optimistically claim is the source of the name Elvis.

Some trace of St. Elvis remains in Wales, as not far from the village named Solva on the south Pembrokeshire coast there is a St. Elvis Farm, as well as a neolithic burial chamber that bears the name of St. Elvis Cromlech. Spookily enough, just twenty miles away to the north are the Preseli Hills.

This strange coincidence of the names Elvis and Preseli is not lost on some, who regard it as clear indication that some south Pembrokeshire family did at one time emigrate to North America, adopt the anglicized Presley as their surname, and retain sufficient memory of their Welsh roots to name one of their sons after the saintly Elvis.

Finally, when Elvis died at Graceland in 1977, he is said to have been reading a book about the Holy Shroud of Turin, normally identified as *A Scientific Search for the Face of Jesus* (1972) by Frank O. Adams, which argues that the Turin Shroud really is the burial shroud of Jesus.

Back to St. David of Wales: It is claimed that David lived for over a hundred years, and he died on a Tuesday, March 1 (now

St. David's Day). It is generally accepted that this was around the year 589. The monastery is said to have been "filled with angels as Christ received his soul." His last words to his followers were in a sermon on the previous Sunday: "Be joyful, and keep your faith and your creed. Do the little things that you have seen me do and heard about. I will walk the path that our fathers have trod before us." "Do the little things" is today a very well-known phrase in Welsh, and has proved an inspiration to many.

Elvis Presley never performed in his ancestral homeland, but fans still talk fondly of the 60 minutes he spent on Scottish soil at Prestwick airport in 1960 on his way home from national service in Germany. For further evidence of his affinity for Scotland, they point out that he once sang *Auld Lang Syne*:

> *Should auld acquaintance be forgot*
> *and never brought to mind*
> *Should auld acquaintance be forgot*
> *And days of auld lang syne*
>
> *For auld lang syne, my dear*
> *For auld lang syne*
> *We'll take a cup of kindness yet*
> *For auld lang syne*

A good English translation of the words *auld lang syne* is "times gone by." So, I realize it's a bit of a stretch, my friends, but it just goes to show ya: In the end it's *all* church history. We're *all* connected to church history—even Elvis.

Thank-ya-ver'-much.

Ortho-Man!

Some of you may be surprised to learn that Houston, Texas, is a burgeoning market for Hollywood-style big-budget-production movies. With big money to be made with summer offerings of fantastic heroes like Iron Man, Indiana Jones, Speed Racer, Superman, Spiderman, and the Hulk, it was only a matter of time before someone came up with the idea of an Orthodox superhero. And, wouldn't you know, they'd choose to film it in Houston!

We've got a gal in our parish who works with such projects, and she asked if I'd like to be a consultant. My role would be to view some of the scenes already in production, help out with proposed scenes, etc. "Sure," I said. I mean, who wouldn't?

All night the night before, I kept imagining what I might expect to find on the set of *Ortho-Man!* I thought back to my own childhood, back before God created color, back in the days of black & white:

Look! Up in the sky! It's a bird! It's a plane!
It's **Superman!**

Maybe, in the spirit of Orthodox unity and all, I could expect:

Look! There in the altar! It's a Greek! It's an Arab! It's a Slav!
(He ain't heavy, he's a convert—he's my brother!)
It's **Ortho-Man!**

That was kind of silly. But it was not nearly as silly as what I found the next day when I was ushered onto the set of *Fr. Bob and the*

Bad Hair Day. That's right; as we walked onto the set where the film-ing was taking place, I learned that the movie being made was called *Fr. Bob and the Bad Hair Day.*

"No, no, no," I said, "this'll never do!"

"What?" answered Genie, my guide.

"*Fr. Bob and the Bad Hair Day!*"

"Oh," she said, "that's not the Orthodox production. See, to cut costs we're sharing film crews and venues with the Roman Catho-lics and the Protestants. *Fr. Bob and the Bad Hair Day* is the Roman Catholic movie."

"Hmmm," I said. "What's the Protestant movie called?"

"I think it's called, *Call No Man 'Father' & Your Hair Will Look Just Fine!*"

"But—that sounds like—"

"Oh, I'm just kidding," she replied, "but you know how the Prots are always reacting to Rome; some things never change."

That said, I was almost scared to ask, but I did: "What's the Orthodox movie called? I assume it's not *Ortho-Man!*"

"No, silly," she said, "it's called *Father Barsanuphios is One Bad Hairy Dude. Just* kidding; but we did, briefly, consider plagiarizing that old Spiderman theme song:

"Ortho-Man, Ortho-Man
Does whatever a Cath'lic can
His name is Gleb, in disguise
Brings in sheaves, smashes lies
Look out! Here comes the Ortho-Man!"

As my guide was finishing the failed theme song, we bumped into Scott Riddle, who was their gopher on the set. Scott said, "We've got to get one of those white tab thingies—you know, the things the priests wear, looks like a tongue depressor?"

"Sure, Scott," Genie said. "Maybe the Catholic crew can lend you one."

To my shock, Genie informed me that the little white tab thingy was one of Ortho-Man's special weapons. Imagine: *whuw-whuw-whuw-whuw-whuw! Bee-yang!* Like a flying blade.

Before I could protest—I mean, not all American Orthodox clergy wear tab shirts—she seemed to read my mind, adding, "I know what you're thinking—'Why not dress Ortho-Man in a cassock?' You ever tried running in a dress? How 'bout flying?"

"But—"

"But, nothing. Listen, early on we had Ortho-Man in a *klobuk*— you know, the long black headdress thing monks and bishops wear? But we nixed the idea when the old-timers said it looked too much like Sally Field in the old TV series, *The Flying Nun.*"

At this point, I admit, I was aghast; I started taking notes.

"Oh! Did they tell you?" she said: "Ortho-Man has a sidekick: the Demon Deacon!"

I stammered, "You. Are. Kidding. Right?"

"Not at all! You know that cool vestment thingy the deacon has that hangs down from one shoulder?"

"Yes—the orarion."

"Whatever. In the movie, that's used like a lasso to capture the bad guys!" she squealed.

I was starting to get a bad feeling about all this when around the corner came a man they called the Grim Reaper because he was always bearing bad news. "We need a can opener! Hello?! Who was supposed to get the can opener?" He was carrying a big can of spinach.

My guide saw my confused look and said, "Ortho-Man's super-human power source."

"That's like Popeye," I said.

"Exactly. They're kin to each other, related," Genie said, "Popeye and Ortho-Man. Don't you think Popeye was probably Greek? I mean, he was a sailor and all."

That was news to me, Popeye being Greek. I asked, "Okay, what about the Hulk?"

"Of course he's Russian," she said. "Oh! And, before we settled on the movie's theme song, we'd even considered basing it on Popeye's:

"I'm Nik'lai the Ortho-Man,
I'm Nik'lai the Ortho-Man.
I'm tough on the sin-age
Cause I eats me spinach.
I'm Nik'lai the Ortho-Man.

"Speaking of which, were you aware that the second verse of the Popeye song includes these words . . .

"I'm one tough gazookus
Which hates all palookas

"Now you know with words like *gazookus* and *palookas*," Genie said, "Popeye's gotta be Orthodox, probably Greek!"

"Popeye's a cartoon character," I said, "not exactly a superhero."

"What's the difference?" she asked.

"Hmmm," I thought, "what *is* the difference between a superhero and a cartoon character?"

Before I could answer, we entered a darkened room where they were screening a couple of scenes of the new movie for editing.

All you need is love—whaah-wha-wha-wha whaaah . . .

"What's this?" I asked.

All you need is love—whaah-wha-wha-wha whaaah . . .

"I think it's the Beatles, 1967," said Genie.

whaah-wha-wha-wha whaaah . . .

"No, I mean—"

"Wait! You're right! This can't be right," she said. "Let's get out of here."

Love, love . . . Love is all you need . . .

"Whew!" Genie gasped as we exited, "wrong screening. That was the Protestant movie!"

As we made our way toward another screening room, we were passed by several interesting characters that had recently been either added or discarded from the script. First, there was Acrivia Man. Acrivia Man was very much about following the rules and canons to a fault. In the end, the moviemakers deemed he might be a hard pill to swallow for the summer audience.

Then there was Economia Man. Economia Man, sort of the opposite of Acrivia Man, was good at jumping through hoops, doing the limbo, and, curiously enough, walking backwards. He, too, was cut from the script after the powers that be deemed him too loose for some, not loose enough for others; so they had to let him loose.

As we made our way toward the room for the screening of *Ortho-Man!* we passed by one other screening where some folks were watching segments of the Roman Catholic film. I poked my head in and it looked so confusing. Honestly, I couldn't tell if it was supposed to be a church film or not. It seemed so chaotic.

I asked, "How do they make sense of it all?"

Genie said, "They don't. They flash subliminal photos of the pope onto the screen, just for a split second, about every 45 seconds, and no matter what chaos may be enveloping the church, Roman Catholics feel much better and at peace just knowing that the pope is there."

Finally, we arrived at Studio Three, where they were screening portions of the upcoming summer blockbuster starring the Orthodox superhero, *Ortho-Man!*

But before we go on, think about it: What would an Orthodox superhero do? What evils might an Orthodox superhero battle in America? Are these within the Church? Without? Or both?

Ortho-Man & the Confusion of Tongues

There's a guy named Smith who produces the Ortho-dixie podcast. After the first installment of **Ortho-Man!** he wrote me, saying, "I didn't put 'Part 1' on it since I figured you'd have a splashy title next week, something like 'Ortho-Man Returns' or 'Ortho-Man 2: The Byzantine Empire Strikes Back'—but, isn't Ortho-Man the guy who sprayed my apartment for ants?" And then, Producer Smith added, " 'Illinois Smith and the Temple of Ortho' has a nice ring to it."

Believe me, when I solicited views from the Ancient Faith Radio audience concerning Ortho-Man, I had no idea what I was getting myself into. Just for fun, I've incorporated all of those emails into this second part.

Just a refresher: In the studio, in order to cut costs, the Orthodox moviemakers were sharing a building with other Christian groups. The Roman Catholics were making a movie called "Fr. Bob and the Bad Hair Day," the Protestants were making a movie called "Call No Man 'Father' & Your Hair Will Look Just Fine!" And the Orthodox were making a movie which, I had assumed, was called none other than: **Ortho-Man!**

So there I was with my guide, Genie, when the theatre lights darkened, and on the screen, just like in the real movies, they showed a trailer of an upcoming feature: a strange movie in which the superhero wore a toga and a garland around his head, and sported golden skin. This superhero fed on a steady diet of lamb, grapes, and olive oil, all the while battling the evil forces that bedeviled him. Those of you who are fans of comic book heroes have no doubt guessed it . . . It was *Hellas Boy II*. ("Hellas" as in Greek for "Greece.")

Anyway, it was time for the opening scene of *OrthoMan!* First, the theme song, which was kind of a rip-off, but the music sounded exactly like the music for Darth Vader in *Star Wars*—*Bom Bom Bom bum buh Bommm bum buh Bommm . . .*

Eis polla eti Despota . . .

Eis polla eti Despota . . .

As the song continued, an evil-looking bishop appeared on the screen. I started to get a queasy feeling. I didn't like it. Then the bishop spoke.

Y'all, I didn't understand a word he said! I objected, "Wait a minute! What is this, the Greek version?"

They stopped the film. "Fr. Joseph," the director said, "we are trying to make an authentic film about an Orthodox superhero. For your information, that's not Greek. The majority of the world's Orthodox Christians speak and understand Russian. I take it you don't?"

"A little," I said. "But you *are* going to have subtitles in the final production, aren't you?"

"Absolutely," he lied.

"What do the bad guys speak?" I asked.

"Arabic, of course!" he cried.

No sir, I didn't like this at all. *Haram.* Anyway, the mean ol' bishop was devising a plan to cause turmoil within the American Orthodox Church. The plan was to encourage hard-and-fast cultural differences, all the while downplaying the need for evangelism: keep the Greeks, Greek; the Russians, Russian; the Serbs, Serb; and the Arabs—well heck, come to think of it, he didn't mention the Arabs, for, as with all current movies, they were portrayed as non-Christian militant religious fanatics.

My mind was swimming with all the things I saw wrong with the project when I heard, *Psssssssssssst!* Like someone trying to get my attention.

I looked back at the movie screen just in time to see a rock go ripping through it. I thought, "Wow! Obviously some sort of 3D action!" But the gasps from the gathered moviemakers and, of course, the big gaping hole in the middle of the movie screen led me to understand otherwise. Someone had hurled a stone at the *Ortho-Man!* preview.

Looking up toward the balcony, I saw a shadowy figure in a cape. I turned to Genie and asked, "Is it Ortho-Man?"

"No," she said, "it looks like disgruntled former co-star, Acrivia Man."

"Acrivia Man?" I said, squinting up at him. "But why?"

"He hates movies. I mean, that's the main reason we had to let him go."

"I don't, er, hmm. I don't understand."

Psssssssssssst!

There it was again.

"Did you hear that?" I asked Genie.

"Hear what?" she said.

About that time more rocks tore through the movie screen. One struck a crew member, and one bounced right off the stage and—*POW!*—hit me square in the head, right between the eyes. It knocked me flat out!

Psssssssssssst!

Suddenly, I no longer noticed the pain from the rock and, stranger still, I found myself sitting on a bus when the outline for a quick story with an Orthodox superhero laid itself out before me. It resembled my readings of the lives of the saints and my thinking, "Someone from the outside might think these men and women to be superheroes in the way that Barnabas and Paul were called 'gods' in Lystra when they performed their works."

In my fantasy I figured the heroes would be a pair of monks (because a Christian alone can do nothing but perish, right?). One would be an elder who lived in the desert in the early centuries of the Church. He became so filled with the power of Christ that he would literally live John 14:12: "Most assuredly, I say to you, he who believes in Me, the works that I do he will do also; and greater works than these he will do, because I go to My Father." He would be dressed as a simple monastic (which, in a movie, hopefully won't be mistaken for a Jedi knight), and would perform all the gifts of the Holy Spirit that would be good for a superhero, such as healing, prophecy, raising the dead, multiplying gifts, speaking in all languages, moving mountains, and time-traveling.

So we see our elder in ancient times being asked to help the people that come to see him, which of course he does. At some point, a widow asks him to find her lost boy. He can see the child is dying in the desert, and so asks God for help in finding and saving the young boy. He is suddenly given the ability to travel through space and time to find this person before he dies. He brings him back. After this, he allows himself to be used by God to travel wherever and whenever he is needed most.

Then enters the sidekick (in the present time) in some bad situation where he needs help. The elder, deep in prayer, suddenly appears—*bang!*—out of thin air, and saves the young man from his apparent doom. Hijinks begin as the rebellious young man pledges himself to the elder. (After all, a movie needs some comical elements; though I'm not sure how comical monastic training would end up being in the end.)

Ahem . . .

Y'all? You know how it feels when you're asleep, but not quite totally, and not fully awake? I was feeling kind of groggy, my head was throbbing a bit. Then I remembered an email I received after I had claimed that Popeye must be Greek. Someone sent me a YouTube video entitled *Greek Mirthology* where Popeye was entertaining his four nephews, Pipeye, Peepeye, Pupeye, and Poopeye, and telling them to eat their spinach so they could be strong like their great, great, great, great uncle Hercules. Truth is, Popeye's—er, I mean, Hercules'—superhuman powers originally were activated by garlic.

GARLIC!

"If it was garlic that made him strong, when did the spinach pipe come along?" the nephews asked.

One day, Bluto the bully put some chlorophyll on his garlic clove and made it wilt. Then he punched Popeye, who landed open-mouthed in a field of spinach, after consumption of which he became a man of steel.

Bluto: "How come you got strength without garlic?
Popeye: "Better'n garlic is spinach!"

And then . . .

I thought of another type of Orthodox superhero. He would be a man who in this world already had some, but not all, of the abilities of the renovated man that will exist after the Resurrection. However, he would live not in a world like ours but in a world with "superhero logic." Basically, our man would have found Eden, and there the Tree of Life. To his surprise, there are only ten fruits there, representing the ten commandments of God, but also the divine virtues. He is given the grace of eating just one tiny bit of a fruit he may choose. Because he has been wronged in the past, he chooses the fruit of justice. Of course, after eating of it, he learns that revenge has nothing to do with divine justice, but he acquires powers the same way to fight injustice wherever it raises its evil horns.

I thought of Hellas Boy II . . . Popeye . . . Illinois Smith . . . Tom & Jerry . . . *Wait.* Tom & Jerry? I must have been dreaming!

Pssssssssssssst!

There it was again—*Pssssssssssssst!*—and I could smell garlic. But we'll get back to the story of Ortho-Man in a moment.

First, I need to mention an email I received which stated that Andrei Tarkovsky made a comment regarding his movie *Andrei Rublev*, something like: The artist does not work in ideal conditions; the hardships bring out the work. I think it is true about Christian life, not just the artist's life. More generally, I think the main problem for Orthodox Christians in the US is the focus on "being right" instead of relying on Christ, on fixing the Church's "mistakes" before knowing Christ, on bringing the truth to others before having a relationship with the Truth.

The email continued: Maybe Ortho-Man should fight the Yankees—I mean, if one jurisdiction tries to impose on others their own way of doing things, that might be considered an invasion!

Heh!

Ortho-Man & the Riddle of the Psssssssssssst!

*****Growing up in the sixties and seventies,***** *I was a fan of the Batman TV series, in which every episode was usually continued to the next one with Batman and Robin only inches away from being sawn in two, gassed into a stupor, eaten by sharks, canceled by network executives, or some such. However, concerning the making of* **Ortho-Man!** *nothing quite so dramatic has happened.*

Earlier we saw an image of a menacing-looking bishop whose plan was to encourage hard-and-fast cultural differences, all the while downplaying the need for evangelism within the American Orthodox Church: keep the Greeks, Greek; the Russians, Russian; the Serbs, Serb, and the Arabs—well, always portray them as non-Christian militant religious fanatics. (And American converts? I assume they can flounder—Lord knows they're crazy, but at least they tithe.)

Then, just as that first scene of **Ortho-Man!** *was being screened, chaos ensued as a disgruntled former employee, Acrivia Man, threw rocks, tearing the movie screen and, seemingly, knocking unconscious yours truly. Then there was that mysterious person somewhere in the back of the darkened theater who kept going: Psssssssssssst! Psssssssssssst! That's where we shall continue, in the finale of* **Ortho-Man!**

There it was again—*Psssssssssssst!* I could smell garlic. And then I found myself following the mysterious figure down a dark hallway. The only light emanated from the candle the hooded figure carried.

"Enjoying your movie?" he asked.

"Well, I don't know," I replied, "it's all in a foreign language."

"Some people will understand it," he said.

"Oh sure," I said, "but not Americans. We're linguistically lazy for the most part, only having learned our native tongue. Hey, who are you?"

"That's not important," he said. "What is important can be found on these walls."

"Walls?" I hadn't even noticed. But, much like Walls of Fame found in universities or halls of government, featuring various VIPs, the walls of the dark hallway through which we were passing were covered with paintings and black-and-white photos of—well, I wasn't quite sure.

"These paintings and old photos—who are these people?" I asked.

"These," he said, "are the real Ortho-Men, males & females."

"Saints?"

"Sure, some of them, perhaps all—only God knows," he replied.

I stopped for a moment and, borrowing his candle, held it up to an old sepia-tone photo of immigrants, shopkeepers, steel mill workers, jiddos and yayas, moms, pops, and grands, lives of struggle etched on their faces—simple, common, everyday people.

While I was downstairs making my way through a dark tunnel with what's-his-face, upstairs chaos reigned. Through the tear in the screen caused by the projectile from Acrivia Man, both the Roman Catholics and the Protestants were looking in on the fight that had broken out among the Orthodox filmmakers. But more on that later . . .

I asked my hooded guide, "Just who is Acrivia Man?"

"Oh, you mean Hypocrite Man," he said.

"Hypocrite Man?"

"Well, that's what I call him. His real name is Kyle Judson. He's a recent convert to Orthodoxy who feels it necessary to save the True Faith from creeping modernity and, to his mind, heresy," he said.

I said, "He's an actor?"

"Yes," said the guide. "He's an actor opposed to acting, citing ancient church canons against attending the theatre. It seems the rules apply to everyone but him. Thus, in truth, he should be called Hypocrite Man rather than Acrivia Man."

My guide continued, "*Acrivia* means 'strict exactitude'—holding to the letter of the law or canons."

"But there was another actor they let go who was known as Economia Man. What's his deal?"

Mr. Mysterious replied, "He, too, is an imposter. Economy (*oikonomía*) refers to a 'dispensation.' Whereas *acrivia* refers to the exact application of canon law, *economy* refers to an exemption or dispensation from some aspect of a canon by the bishop or some other clergyman (depending on the matter at hand) for the purpose of promoting the salvation of one or many persons. Unlike Acrivia Man, a stereotype of American converts, Economia Man was raised in the Orthodox Faith and now has fashioned his own views along cultural lines, distorting the True Faith (or, in his case, good acting in general)."

"I don't get it," I said.

He looked at me a moment, but due to the darkness I still couldn't make out his features. He said, "Name your favorite superheroes, cartoon or action characters, and tell me *why* they are your favorites."

"As a kid I liked Underdog because I pull for underdogs. Later, it was the Pink Panther because he was so cool, nothing disturbed his peace. But my real biggie-big as a kid was Batman. He looked menacing, but fought injustice. He taught me that a character is not always to be judged by his looks.

"I saw the first Indiana Jones movie back when I was in college and it so thrilled me that I ran all the way back to the dorm and called my parents and told them they had to go to movies!"

"Why?" he asked.

"Because it made my spirit soar!" I said.

"To infinity and beyond?" he quipped.

"No. That was yet to come with Buzz Lightyear. I love Buzz!"

"Why?" he said.

"Because," I replied, "Buzz never gives up hope. Even though he has limitations, he never lets that keep him from flying, from serving, from helping. I guess I'm a fan of Buzz Lightyear because of his honesty."

"Bingo," he said.

"Bingo?" I replied. "You mean like the dog, *B-I-N-G-O*?"

"No," he said. "I mean 'Bingo' as in you've hit on the key to being an Ortho-Man."

I looked at him strangely. "Describe your vision of Ortho-Man for me," he said.

I repeated the words that my friend Elijah had sent me in an email:

Ortho-Man wears the super-suit mentioned in Ephesians 6:13–17, the armor of God.

➤ *The waist belt of truth:* its equipment will stop lies about Christians.

➤ *The breastplate of righteousness:* Ortho-man's most powerful weapon, used only when the Orthodox world is almost hopeless.

➤ *The shoes of peace:* a slight kick from the shoes of peace will stop a warfaring enemy.

➤ *The shield of faith:* its defense depends on how many believers are around you.

➤ *The helmet of salvation:* with this on, you can catch yourself from making a life-changing sin.

➤ *The sword of the spirit:* this sword will deliver hard, stunning blows filled with Christ's power!

"Nice," he said. "But essentially, Ortho-Man is clothed with Christ. Everything you admire about the created superheroes and action figures, as long as it is true, is to be found in Christ."

"What do you mean, as long as it's true? All of those superheroes and action characters are, well, make-believe," I replied.

"Yes, but our spirits wouldn't soar so high if their virtues were built on a lie," he replied.

Pssssssssssssst!

I couldn't see his face clearly, but it was obvious to me now that my mysterious guide was not the one making the *Pssssssssssst!* sound.

Pssssssssssssst!

There it was again.

"You'd better be going," he said.

"Wait! A few more answers, please!"

"Quickly," he said.

"Okay, why is the Orthodox superhero movie being made in a foreign language?"

He said, "That's just your imagination. A temptation, if you will. Don't let language issues distract you from the Truth. Be faithful. Work out your own salvation, in your own language, in your own culture. But realize that until there's Orthodox unity in America, cultures will compete, for good or ill, even within the Church. Nonetheless, struggle well and be faithful.

"St. John Chrysostom said something like: 'A man is no such great lover of the truth, only for holding to it when there is none to lead him astray from it: to hold fast to the truth when many are drawing him away, this makes a proved man.'"

I stared at him for a moment, trying to make out his face, but, strangely, his face was wavering, like it was fading, or rewinding, or morphing. Quickly, I asked, "Like that email I received, stating: 'The main problem for Orthodox Christians in America is the focus on "being right" (instead of relying on Christ), on fixing the Church's "mistakes" before knowing Christ, on bringing the truth to others before having a relationship with the Truth'?"

"Exactly," he said. "Economia & acrivia serve the Church, not vice versa. Save your soul. Don't be a hypocrite."

Pssssssssssssst!

Someone was shaking my arm; the man before me was fading. "Wait!"

Psssssssssssst!

My head was hurting. As if waking from a dream, I opened my eyes, expecting to see the chaotic scene of Orthodox moviemakers fighting among themselves. But to my great surprise, I saw—unbelievable! It was a scene in the movie where the apostles were portrayed proclaiming the Good News, and everyone in the theatre could hear it in his own language!

We all sat there for a moment, Orthodox, non-Orthodox, even nonbelievers, and wondered at the sight: "Their sound hath gone forth into all the earth. And their words unto the ends of the world."

In the movie it was Pentecost and the disciples were all together in one place:

When the Day of Pentecost had fully come, they were all with one accord in one place. And suddenly there came a sound from heaven, as of a rushing mighty wind, and it filled the whole house where they were sitting. Then there appeared to them divided tongues, as of fire, and one sat upon each of them. And they were all filled with the Holy Spirit and began to speak with other tongues, as the Spirit gave them utterance.

And there were dwelling in Jerusalem Jews, devout men, from every nation under heaven. And when this sound occurred, the multitude came together, and were confused, because everyone heard them speak in his own language. Then they were all amazed and marveled, saying to one another, "Look, are not all these who speak Galileans? And how is it that we hear, each in our own language in which we were born? Parthians and Medes and Elamites, those dwelling in Mesopotamia, Judea and Cappadocia,

Pontus and Asia, Phrygia and Pamphylia, Egypt and the
parts of Libya adjoining Cyrene, visitors from Rome, both
Jews and proselytes, Cretans and Arabs—we hear them
speaking in our own tongues the wonderful works of God."
(Acts 2:1–11)

And, from John's Gospel:

On the last day, that great day of the feast, Jesus stood and
cried out, saying, "If anyone thirsts, let him come to Me
and drink. He who believes in Me, as the Scripture has said,
out of his heart will flow rivers of living water." But this He
spoke concerning the Spirit, whom those believing in Him
would receive; for the Holy Spirit was not yet given, because
Jesus was not yet glorified. (John 7:37–39)

Then Jesus spoke to them again, saying, "I am the light of
the world. He who follows Me shall not walk in darkness,
but have the light of life." (John 8:12)

And there it was, the revelation, through the Spirit, of the real
Ortho-Man, or to be precise, Ortho-MEN: just simple, common men
and women who have received the Holy Spirit.

Blessed art Thou, O Christ our God, who hast revealed the
fishermen as most wise, having sent upon them the Holy
Spirit, and through them Thou hast fished the universe. O
Lover of mankind, glory to Thee. (Troparion of Pentecost)

So, brothers and sisters in Christ, Ortho-Men, we come to the
end of our tale. Some of you may be wondering about the identity
of *Pssssssssssst* Man. You know, that mysterious person that kept
going, *Pssssssssssst! Pssssssssssst!*
It turned out it was not the mysterious man who revealed to me

Ortho-Man's true identity. Rather, it seems it was none other than my own nagging conscience, with the help of my guardian angel.

You know how sometimes when we're headed down a path of judging our neighbors (be they heathen, brother, or bishop), there's that nagging little voice—*Psssssssssssst!*—that tries to draw us back to the saving reality of the Gospel. Sometimes, forgive me, that pesky *Psssssssssssst!* may just be the prompting of the Holy Spirit, helping to set us free.

Amma Sara of Egypt said, "If I prayed God that all men should approve of my conduct, I should find myself a penitent at the door of each one, but I shall rather pray that my heart may be pure towards all."

Psssssssssssst!

The Xenia-Galina Coinkydink

Years ago, on a Sunday evening, I received a phone call from a man we'll call Tim. At the time, there was a catechumen in our little mission—we'll call her Sherry. The caller said, "Pastor Huneycutt? This is Tim." Thinking the caller to be the Protestant husband, Tim, of the catechumen, Sherry, I said, "Hello, Tim. How are you?"

He said, "Not too good, Pastor—she's gone."

Again, believing I knew those concerned, I said, "Sherry left you?"

He said, "Yes, we had an argument. It got out of hand, and she left."

I started struggling with my words, trying to say the right things, and after about five minutes, he said, "Hey, is this Pastor Huneycutt of Goose Creek Baptist Church?"

I said, "No, uh, I'm sorry. I'm an Orthodox priest."

He apologized; we shared an uncomfortable laugh, and hung up.

I soon learned that there was indeed a Baptist pastor with the last name Huneycutt living in our area. And, what a coincidence, he obviously had a married couple in his parish with the same first names as a couple in my parish.

The story gets even weirder. In those days, I regularly volunteered as a chaplain at a local hospital. About a year or more after the phone episode, during my hospital rounds, for some strange reason, for the first time since it happened, I related that story of the erroneous phone call as I tried to make conversation with a family gathered around the room of a man who was deathly ill. I noticed as I talked that they were not amused; if memory serves me, I threw in some nervous laughter of my own.

When I finished, someone said, "She just left here a moment ago."

"Who just left?" I asked.

"Sherry. She'll be back later, but she had to step out for a while."

I looked at the man lying there and looked back at my list. Sure enough—his name was Tim.

It was coincidence, pure and random. I've found no other way to parse it, all these years since. Sometimes, things just happen that surprise and amaze us by their timing.

For instance, a while back, I was on vacation with my family on the coast of South Carolina. At the risk of causing scandal here, forgive me, but I was "out of uniform" and dressed in shorts and polo shirt. The Huneycutts were waiting for a table in a popular coastal seafood restaurant.

We walked down to the water to look at the shrimp boats, kick and skip rocks, and all the normal time-occupiers employed in such instances. My youngest daughter was wearing a T-shirt from a recent parish life conference in Dallas. It had an outline of the state of Texas on the front. Other patrons were moseying about, waiting on their own tables to open up, and I was a good piece away from the rest of my crew, when I heard a woman say, "Oh, look at her shirt! Are y'all from Texas?"

I heard my wife answer affirmatively. The matriarch exclaimed that her daughter, who was standing there as well, now lived in Texas. As my daughter turned around, the woman saw the other side of the T-shirt and squealed, "And look at that cross! Are y'all Orthodox?"

Now, for those of you unfamiliar with the Carolinas, to hear Southern Anglos talking in such a manner can definitely make one take a closer look, which I did. I saw my wife and kids gathering around this other family of grandparents, kids, grandchildren, and a thirty-something daughter, who now lived in Texas and was Orthodox. I joined the party and my wife said, "Here's my husband, he's out of uniform; he's an Orthodox priest in Houston." They went on to relate how the Orthodox woman had just moved to Dallas from California.

Trying to make conversation, I said, "What parish did you go to in California?" When she told me, I said, "Oh, my boss's sister is a nun there."

I told her the name and her jaw dropped a bit; she said, "Oh, I know her well!"

The matriarch, with a noticeable Southern twang, said, "But she grew up near Charlotte. That's where we live."

I said, "I grew up near Charlotte—Albemarle."

She said, "Oh! Well, we're from Oakboro!" (There's about 15 minutes between those two rural towns.)

I think everyone could sense that this was getting way too weird for reality and the gathering soon, somewhat slack-jawed, dispersed. You just never know. I wondered, had I been dressed in a cassock, if this family would even have approached us. In the end, at least as far as I can discern, it was just a random encounter that, truth be known, probably happens more often than we realize. We've all probably experienced coincidences that present deeper meaning—times when we can see God moving in our lives—which brings me to the story of a woman from the former Soviet Union named Galina.

Galina moved to the States after marrying a Southern man and settled in the foothills of North Carolina. Naturally, being Russian Orthodox, though she lived an hour and a half away from the church, she began to worship with us, but only on occasion. That all changed when she discovered, at the age of 37, that she had cancer. It was then, when she was facing death, that we saw Galina increase her attendance at church.

Though she lived an hour and a half away, "down the mountain," she was there most every Sunday: confessing, praying, communing, and, quite frankly, glowing. Though she eventually lost her hair and became gaunt, when Galina entered the church it was like a presence was among us. It was a transformation that's hard to explain.

Her English was pretty good, but there were times when she had trouble finding the right word. Once, while visiting her in her home, I apologized for my lack of Russian.

I said, "I'm sorry, about all I know is *Gospodi pomilui.*"

Without hesitation, sweetly, she said, "Then you know the most important part."

To hear someone so young dying of cancer say, with all sincerity, that knowing "Lord, have mercy" in Russian is the most important part is humbling. I had many opportunities—we all did in those days—to appreciate humility, thanks to Galina.

Now we come to the inexplicable part, the part that still shadows me, especially when my own faith is weak. But first a little back story. Years ago, during a clergy conference, another priest and I were staying with a Russian couple in Washington, DC. After dinner, the woman, who worked for the government and used to make frequent trips to the Soviet Union, related the following story.

She said, back in the bad old days of the Soviet Union there was a code among decent folks to prevent unwarranted suspicion by the authorities. That is, if you were to deliver a message to someone, say, in an office, you might ask, "Is Tonya here?" And, though the person you were asking was she, you might be told, "No, but have a seat and she will be with you shortly." This was the reply if the coast was not clear.

This woman related how she went to deliver a message to just such a recipient one day, and the woman behind the desk, sensing another was approaching, asked the woman from the US government to have a seat. It was at this point that another woman, in a great state of distress, burst into the office claiming that the authorities were coming. She was carrying a box of old jars full of oil.

She then told them that these came from the shrine to St. Xenia of St. Petersburg. When she'd heard that the authorities were coming to close down the shrine, she had gone inside and drained all the hanging oil lamps of their oil and collected it in these jars. She asked the woman behind the desk if there was a safe place to keep them. That's when the American lady spoke up and said, "I can take them back to America with me." With gratitude the Russian lady, who was very devoted to the memory of St. Xenia of St. Petersburg, gave the American woman the box full of collected oil from the lampadas at St. Xenia's shrine.

As this lady related her story that evening in our nation's capital, I couldn't help but notice that her husband had been dispensing oil from a jar into a small glass container. The couple sent me home with a small vial of the oil to take back to our little Orthodox mission in North Carolina.

Galina later died what I consider a good death. That is, she was able to confess and commune up until her final days, and she had the full prayers of the unction service prayed over her and was anointed shortly before her death.

On one of my last visits to her, as I was preparing to travel down the mountain, I paused as I stood before a shelf by the prothesis that contained various oils and holy keepsakes. At first, I grabbed the oil of unction. Then I turned back, placed it back on the shelf, picked up the oil from St. Xenia's lamps, and dropped it into my riassa pocket. Even as I put it in my pocket I thought, "Why are you taking this?"

This is a true story, and I hope you, dear reader, will forgive me, but, seriously, all the way down the mountain to Galina's I had this nagging thought: "Why did you put the oil of unction back and bring the St. Xenia oil?"

As was our custom, I entered Galina's bedroom (she'd been bedridden for some time), and confessed and communed her. As I reached into my riassa and pulled out the vial of oil, I noticed a tiny icon I'd never seen before on her wall. As I tipped the oil onto my thumb, I asked, "Is this an icon of your patron, St. Galina?"

"Yes, Father," Galina said. "But I don't know much about her. My favorite saint, the one I pray to every day, the one who has helped me so much in my struggle with cancer, the one who has visited me, is St. Xenia of St. Petersburg. Do you know her?"

I stood there with the oil of St. Xenia's lamp on my thumb and my jaw on the floor. Honestly, I don't remember what happened first: Did I anoint her and then tell her about the oil, or vice versa?

Suffice it to say, I was very excited. Galina, however, was just as calm and peaceful as could be. She was not surprised at all. So great was her faith. So weak was mine. Coincidence? I don't think so.

There's an old saying: "Coincidence is God's way of remaining anonymous." I no longer believe that. With the host of saints who've gone before us, and through their heavenly intercessions, how can God remain anonymous?

True, like the mix-up on Pastor Huneycutt's name in the phone book and the retelling of the same to the caller himself; like bumping into someone a thousand miles away who is as close as a sister in Christ: some coincidences lack gravitas. Then there are stories like this of St. Xenia, which, in a very circuitous way, comforts a dying Russian woman in the foothills of North Carolina. God is wondrous in His saints.

Blessed Xenia was happily married to a colonel, a court singer, in St. Petersburg. It is assumed that she came from a prominent family. When Xenia was only twenty-six years old, her husband suddenly died at a drinking party. This unexpected blow so shocked Xenia that it completely changed her way of looking at life. Understanding that her husband had not prepared himself for death, Xenia became consumed with the eternal state of her beloved's soul. She no longer went to parties or visited with friends. She gave away all her belongings to the poor. Her total denial of worldly things, along with her wearing her dead husband's clothes and insisting folks call her by his name, Andrew, led her family to think she was crazy. Xenia became dead to the world.

She prayed outside the city gates at night, in inclement weather.

She also secretly helped to build the Smolensk cemetery church—leaving piles of bricks for the morning workmen. And, although ridiculed, laughed at, and scorned, Xenia bore the taunts and prayed for the souls of those who hurled them. Eventually, however, people began to see the otherworldly sanctity of Blessed Xenia and the extraordinary gifts, even clairvoyance, that God had bestowed on her.

Blessed Xenia died at the end of the eighteenth century, at the age of 71. Her grave became a place of pilgrimage, even through the Soviet period, though for several decades the political authorities closed the chapel at her gravesite. (This is where the oil came from.)

Even the words of the Church's hymn to St. Xenia of St. Petersburg provide a lesson for the living and comfort for the dying:

In you, O mother, was carefully preserved what is according to the image,
For you took up the cross and followed Christ.
By so doing, you taught us to disregard the flesh, for it passes away,
But to care instead for the soul since it is immortal.
Therefore, O Blessed Xenia, your spirit rejoices with the angels.

Although my parishioner, Galina, found strength from her relationship with St. Xenia, it would seem to have been a cooperative exercise—for in the Smolensk cemetery, on St. Xenia's tombstone are written these words: "Whoever has known me, may he remember my soul for the salvation of his own soul."

It's events like this one, dear reader, which help to fortify our faith, making that giant leap one well worth the effort (all of it). Fall down, get back up, fall down, get back up—and, if I may be so bold: *Shut up, go home, pray more.*

Through the prayers of St. Xenia of St. Petersburg and all the saints, may God be merciful to us and save us!

Back Story

······························

Shut Up, Go Home, Pray More
The Not of This World Conference sponsored by Rose Hill College and *Touchstone* magazine—Aiken, South Carolina, May 1995—was, hands down, the best theological gathering I have ever attended. Humble thanks to Don "Athanasius" Wiley of Johnson City, Tennessee, for making it possible.

> ***More on the Not of This World Conference:*** http://www.touchstonemag.com/ archives/article.php?id=10-03-027b (4/17/09)
>
> ***Jaroslav Pelikan quote:*** http://en.wikipedia.org/wiki/Jaroslav_Pelikan (4/17/09)

What It Takes
This podcast bubbled up from out of nowhere; yet it is undeniably autobiographical. For some reason I always hear the Beatles, "He's a real nowhere man, sitting in his nowhere land," when I think of this episode.

American Orthodoxy?
It's just plain sin that keeps Orthodox Christians administratively divided in America. God willing, episodes such as this one (most of this book, even) will one day be outdated.

> ***Fr. Aris Metrakos's article:*** http://www/orthodoxytoday.org/articles6/ MetrakosAmerica.php (4/17/09)

The Great Orthodox Awakening
It's the American Way: "Now that I've found a viable product, how best to market it?" This podcast is not a criticism of creativity. Rather, it serves as a reminder that humility cannot be marketed, only lived.

Hello Jiddo, Hello Yaya
Many thanks to Fr. Alexis Duncan, Uncle Paul Finley, Gayle Malone, and Fr. James Shadid for allowing me to experience Orthodox church camp as a priest, counselor, and camper. Much like our life in Christ, it can't be fully explained, only lived. Church camp is life-changing.

> ***The anonymously penned camp letter:*** Often referred to as the *Boy Scout Letter from Camp*, it is found in various forms and sites on the Internet [e.g., http://www/gcfl.net/archive.php?funny=19990310 (4/17/09)]
>
> ***Make your own camp letter:*** http://grantmcl.tripod.com/letter.html (4/17/09)

Alan Sherman's classic **Hello Muddah, Hello Fadduh:** http://www.oldielyr-
ics.com/lyrics/allan_sherman/hello_muddah_hello_fadduh_a_letter_
from_camp.html (4/17/09)

Orthodox Christian Anarchist at Large

The trouble plaguing the Orthodox Church in America, broadcast on the Internet
in 2005–2008, was the catalyst for this material. From time to time, however, all
communities are prone to the mischief wrought by a disgruntled few. We must bear
in mind that weaker brethren are sorely tempted (which applies equally to all).

> Kenneth C. Haugk, *Antagonists in the Church—How to Identify and Deal with
> Destructive Conflict* (Minneapolis: Augsburg Publishing House, 1988), pp.
> 20, 72, 38–39.

> "Sometimes at night, when I am saying my prayers . . ."—A. Darwin Kirby,
> Jr., *Jottings—Easily Satisfied with the Best* (Personal Memoir, 1991), p. 121.

Help! There's an Iconostasis in My Living Room!

While on vacation in the summer of 2007 my family, normally deprived of television, became addicted to makeover shows while viewing other people's TV sets. I
never quite got it, till this (very real) idea came to mind. May God bless the mission priest!

> **"Rocky Raccoon" lyrics:** http://www/sing365.com/music/lyric.nsf/Rocky-
> Raccoon-lyrics-The-Beatles/96E6311ECBFA360048256BC2002114C2
> (4/17/09)

Orthodox White Boy

Save teasers on the Orthodixie blog, rarely do I encourage folks to listen to a particular podcast. This episode was an exception. I loved it. Forgive me, but it was fun
to write, record, and listen to. As a white boy, I never experienced being part of a
minority until becoming Orthodox. I'm glad the majority lets guys like me in!

> **Fr. James Bernstein**: the author of *Surprised by Christ: My Journey from
> Judaism to Orthodox Christianity:* http://www.surprisedbychrist.com/
> (4/17/09)

Fasters Anonymous

I was blessed to have worked for two years in a substance abuse recovery center. I
enjoyed, appreciated—and miss—the honest lessons learned in Twelve Step gath-
erings, especially the open meetings for Narcotics Anonymous. May God help us
all, one day at a time, to recover from the results of the Fall which, like the Savior
Himself, hound us all.

> **St. John Chrysostom quotes:** http://www.orthodoxytoday.org/articles4/
> ChrysostomFasting.php (4/17/09)

E.I.E.I.O.

Fasting takes its toll on the mind, the body, the spirit, and the ol' patience fuse.
Using a non-writeable sound (finger, lips, hum, up and down)—*e.i.e.i.o*—was the

only way I could politely convey what many of us suffer during the latter days of festal preparation. Those who've been there know exactly what I mean. Those who have not, well, let's just all pray for each other.

> Bishop Ignatius Brianchaninov, *The Arena—An Offering to Contemporary Monasticism,* trans. Archimandrite Lazarus (Jordanville, New York: Holy Trinity Monastery), p. 122.
>
> **A source for the Tuesday Cheese week hymn:** http://www/churchyear.net/prelent.html

Two Miles till Pascha

My Pastoral Theology professor, Fr. Charles Caldwell, always said, "Trust the process." That's the back story on this episode. The process toward the Feast of Feasts, Pascha, is one that is trodden with trust, not in ourselves but in the Good God who saves us.

Baby Jesus by the Chimney

For years, Orthodox columnist Terry Mattingly ran a series on the Christmas Wars—which got me thinking, "What's it really all about, anyway?"

> **A source for the red wagon story:** httpss://www.goofball.com/jokes/misc/INC20071225041843 (4/17/09)
>
> **Nativity Kontakion:** http://www.churchyear.net/nathymns.html (4/17/09)

The Ghost of Past Christmas Presents

Garth Brooks sang, "Sometimes I thank God for unanswered prayers." Then again, the prayers that *are* answered, by God Himself, for those who long for a Savior, even Christ the Lord, are beyond all understanding (and perhaps approachable only in song).

> **Blaise Pascal quote:** http://www.touchstonemag.com/archives/article.php?id=19-10-035-b (4/17/09)
>
> **Shepherds**—Luke 2:15–20

Bending the Rules out of Love

In addition to the folks mentioned in this episode, Archimandrite Damian ("In Memory" at the beginning of the book) was a shining example of someone who bent the rules out of love. Over my years of association with him as spiritual father and friend, I often complained to others of how he would accept back into his good graces those who had previously stabbed him in the back; it was a noticeable "flaw" of his. Then again, having been on the other end of the knife, forgive me, I've also been known to say that I hope God's a lot like Fr. Damian, for He knows I need all the "bending" I can get!

Expect a Miracle!

What can I say, but, "It is good for us to be here." A bishop once said to a gathering of priests, "If we were able to see even the angel that stands vigilant at our church altars we would forever be on our faces in awe." Thanks be to God, normally He acts normally.

Jesus Loves You (But)

The original title for this podcast was "Saved by the Big 'But' of Mercy." Though fitting, grammatically, given our current society's fascination with profanity, better judgment prevailed. It is ironic that many of the folks who told me they appreciated this podcast are some of the "holiest" people I know. Go figure!

Theological BS

The next time you are tempted by road rage, head to the nearest copy of the wonderful children's book by P. D. Eastman called *Go, Dog, Go!* And don't stop there, especially if not cured; head on to the equally wonderful *Grouchy Lady Bug*. In fact, if you live in a traffic-crazy city like Houston, you might want to carry along copies of both books for refresher courses—to be read while parked.

> *Paraphrased quote:* P.D. Eastman, *Go, Dog, Go!* (New York: Beginner Books, 1961), p. 9.
>
> *"Repentance is not a matter of . . ." and "To truly repent . . .":* from Joseph David Huneycutt, *Defeating Sin—Overcoming Our Passions and Changing Forever* (Salisbury, Massachusetts: Regina Orthodox Press, 2007), p. 96.

Bless Your Heart—*Smallah, Smallah, Smallah*!

Ah, yes; the powers we think we have are no match for those actually accessible through God's grace.

> *The Evil Eye:* http://www.geocities/com/Area51/Lair/1729/lebanon.html (4/17/09)

He's in a Better Place . . . than Dixie?

I've never felt comforted at funerals when I hear people say that those who have died are in a better place. I don't know that. But, ignorant though I am, I do know that God is Love—and if the loved one is called home to the Beloved, that's up to Him. Though death is a great mystery, it will never be able to conquer the great mystery of love made manifest in the Incarnation.

> *The Widow of Nain*—Luke 7:11–17
>
> *Jairus' Daughter*—Mark 5:35–43
>
> *The Raising of Lazarus*—John 11:1–45

Letters from the Old Country

Should we thank God for the Old Country? No. We should thank God for the Ark of Salvation, the Church, which for Americans has been preserved and handed down from those from the "Old Country." Really, though, the Old Country ain't never been, and never shall be, Home.

When the Roll Is Called up Yonder

Though I enjoyed the period immensely, I thank God I'm no longer in high school. Greater still shall my thanks ascend if I graduate, instead of flunking, this earthly trial!

> *Quote from Fr. Chad Hatfield:* taken from St. Herman Orthodox Seminary's 2007 Commencement Address (linked source unavailable).

An Empty Church Is a Peaceful Church

This podcast generated the most AFR listener email I've yet received. Don't get me wrong, Fr. Danislav's concerns are real ones that need to be addressed. Yet smashing an egg with a hammer makes for a less-than-perfect omelette (or something like that).

A Funny Thing Happened on the Way to Phronema

This episode was originally broadcast during the week of the Feast of All Saints—which I take to mean those known and unknown—to us. God knows all who have attained phronema. For Him, and them, it's simple.

> ***St. Makarios of Egypt quote:*** Ss. Nikodimos and Makarios, *The Philokalia*, trans. and ed. G.E.H. Palmer, Phillip Sherrard, Kallistos Ware (London: Faber & Faber, 1984), vol. 3, p. 299.
>
> ***St. Maximos the Confessor quote:*** Joanna Manley (ed.), *Grace for Grace, The Psalter and the Holy Fathers* (Menlo Park, California: Monastery Books, 1992), p. 334.

Constantine: He Built the City, but He Didn't Write the Song!

During the hoopla surrounding Dan Brown's book, *The Da Vinci Code,* my supervisor in a North Carolina substance abuse center, Tom Brittain, asked what I thought of the book. I said, "Not much—heretical at worst, spurious at best." He asked if I would write a review of it. I said, "I would never buy a copy!" He said he would lend me his in hopes that I would point out the theological errors. He did, I did, and it was.

I posted a seven-part series on *The Da Vinci Code* on the Orthodixie blog and was later invited to participate (along with other Orthodox authors: Terry Mattingly, Frederica Mathewes-Green, and Fr. Patrick Henry Reardon) in a subcontracted Sony public relations website (now extinct) entitled *The Da Vinci Dialogue*. The site was launched in advance of the movie's release and in anticipation of the expected controversy among Christian consumers. My contribution, assigned by the site editors, was "Who was Constantine the Great?" Portions of that article and of the blog review are included here to provide the historical information on St. Constantine which was gleaned from various sources. It was not by accident that *The Da Vinci Code* movie was released on the feast of St. Constantine the Great, May 19, 2006.

> http://southern-orthodoxy.blogspot.com/2006/05/who-was-constantine-great.html (4/17/09)
>
> ***"Jesus' establishment as 'the Son of God' . . ."***—Dan Brown, *The Da Vinci Code* [*DVC*] (New York: Doubleday, 2003), p. 233.
>
> ***Nicene Council background:*** http://www.envoymagazine.com/planetenvoy/Review-DaVinci-part2-Full.htm (4/17/09)
>
> "Constantine commissioned and financed a new Bible . . ."—*DVC*, p. 234.
>
> ***Tertullian quote:*** http://www.newadvent.org/cathen/04295c.htm (4/17/09)

People for the Ethical Treatment of . . . Dragons?

The icon of St. George slaying the dragon, which, in a parish named St. George, adorns not only the iconostasis but several entryways, invites frequent questions from visitors and inquirers. Digging around for the dirt on the dragon slayer took me to places I'd not anticipated.

> *Sources:*
> http://www.saintgeorgetaybeh.org/html/st_george_story.html (4/17/09)
> http://www.royalsocietyofstgeorge.com/historyofstgeorge.htm (4/17/09)
> http://en.wikipedia.org/wiki/Saint_George (4/17/09)

Saint Elvis?

What credibility would a book by a Southerner have if it mentioned not one word about Elvis? God provides.

> *Article on the thirtieth anniversary of the singer's death:* http://archive.
> newsmax.com/archives/articles/2007/8/17/83406.shtml (4/17/09)
> *Fr. Nicholas Schofield's blog post on Elvis Presley:* http://romanmiscellany.
> blogspot.com/2007/08/five-catholic-facts-about-elvis.html (4/11/09)
> *Lyrics for "Miracle of the Rosary":* http://www.absolutelyrics.com/lyrics/
> view/elvis_presley/miracle_of_the_rosary/
> *St. David of Wales:* http://en.wikipedia.org/wiki/Saint_David (4/17/09)

Ortho-Man! (Parts 1, 2 & 3)

Many AFR listeners contributed to the attributes of Ortho-Man. At one point, I had no idea where the series was going, but having read the lives of the saints, I knew where it had to end up.

> *"A man is no such great lover of the truth . . ."*—Nicene and Post-Nicene
> Fathers of the Christian Church, First Series (Grand Rapids: Eerdmans,
> 1988), vol. 11, p. 210.
> *Amma Sara quote:* http://www.etss.edu/hts/MAPM/info12.htm (4/17/09)

The Xenia–Galina Coinkydink

As all humor must be based in reality, it seemed fitting to end this work on a serious note. If not for the lives of the saints and the pious lives of the faithful, our reality would be, literally, a living hell. Through the prayers of all the saints, may God be merciful to us and save us.

> *Facts on St. Xenia:* http://www.roca.org/OA/43/43m.htm (4/17/09)
> *Hymn to St. Xenia:* http://orthodoxwiki.org/Xenia_of_St._Petersburg
> (4/17/09)

About the Author

Fr. Joseph Huneycutt was reared a Southern Baptist (which, he adds, is a requirement in North Carolina). He spent a decade as an Episcopalian before converting to Orthodoxy in 1993. Fr. Joseph hosts a blog called *Orthodixie* and delivers a weekly podcast on Ancient Faith Radio by the same name. In addition to speaking engagements, retreats, and conferences, Fr. Joseph is best known for his books: *One Flew Over the Onion Dome: American Orthodox Converts, Retreads & Reverts,* and *Defeating Sin: Overcoming Our Passions and Changing Forever.*

Fr. Joseph serves as priest at St. George Antiochian Orthodox Church, Houston, Texas. He and his wife Elizabeth have three children: Mary Catherine, Basil, and Helen; a black cat named Lily; and a black standard poodle named Wotan (Hart).

ANCIENT FAITH RADIO
www.ancientfaithradio.com

Visit www.ancientfaithradio.com to listen to Fr. Joseph Huneycutt's regular podcast, *Orthodixie.*

Other Books of Interest

At the Corner of East and Now
A Modern Life in Ancient Christian Orthodoxy

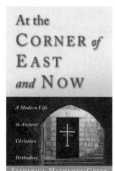

by Frederica Mathewes-Green

Acclaimed author Frederica Mathewes-Green takes us through a typical Divine Liturgy in her little parish of Holy Cross in Baltimore, setting of her well-loved book *Facing East*. Interspersed with reflections on the liturgy and the Orthodox faith are accounts of adventures around the country. In all the places she visits and all the people she meets, Frederica finds insights about faith, American life, and what it means to be human, and she shares these insights with the wit, pathos, and folksy friendliness that have made her one of the most beloved spiritual writers in America.

"A thoughtful source of inspiration for any truth-seeker. . . . If as Mathewes-Green writes, most people have been fed a boiled down 'oatmeal version' of faith, then *At the Corner of East and Now* offers more demanding fare for those with discerning palates." —*Los Angeles Times*

Paperback, 270 pages (ISBN: 978-1-888212-34-1) CP Order No. 007609—$16.95*

Close to Home
One Orthodox mother's quest for patience, peace, and perseverance

by Molly Sabourin

Close to Home is for every young mother who's ever wished children came with an instruction manual; who's ever longed for just one quiet minute to finish a thought or utter a prayer; who's ever despaired of perfecting herself in time to become a good example for her children; who's ever wondered why "happily ever after" takes so darn much work.

With courage, humor, and unflinching honesty, Molly Sabourin addresses all these frustrations and more—offering not answers or solutions, but a new perspective, a pat on the shoulder, a reassuring "I've been there too, and there is hope." Those who share her "quest for patience, peace, and persever-ance" will see themselves in these pages, laugh a little, cry a little, and close the book with new strength to continue the quest.

Paperback, 192 pages (ISBN: 978-1-888212-61-7) CP Order No. 007612—$15.95*

Surprised by Christ
My Journey from Judaism to Orthodox Christianity

by Rev. A. James Bernstein

Surprised by Christ is the story of a man searching for truth and unable to rest until he finds it. Raised in Queens, New York, by formerly Orthodox Jewish parents whose faith had been undermined by the Holocaust, Arnold Bernstein went on his own personal quest for spiritual meaning. He was ready to accept God in whatever form He chose to reveal Himself—and that form turned out to be Christ. But Bernstein soon perceived discrepancies in the various forms of Protestant belief that surrounded him, and so his quest continued—this time for the true Church.

    Surprised by Christ combines an engrossing memoir of one man's life in historic times and situations with an examination of the distinctives of Orthodox theology that make the Orthodox Church the true home not only for Christian Jews, but for all who seek to know God as fully as He may be known.
Paperback, 335 pages (ISBN 978-1-888212-95-2) CP Order No. 007604—$18.95*

Thirsting for God in a Land of Shallow Wells

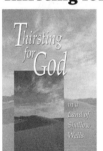

by Matthew Gallatin

Beginning in the street ministry days of the Jesus Movement, Matthew Gallatin devoted more than twenty years to evangelical Christian ministry. He was a singer/songwriter, worship leader, and Calvary Chapel pastor. Nevertheless, he eventually accepted a painful reality: no matter how hard he tried, he was never able to experience the God whom he longed to know. His was a great dream that could not find fulfillment, a deep question that could not answer itself, an eternal thirst dwelling in a land of shallow wells.

    In *Thirsting for God*, Gallatin expresses many of the struggles that a Protestant will encounter in coming face to face with Orthodoxy: such things as Protestant relativism, rationalism versus the Orthodox sacramental path to God, and the unity of Scripture and Tradition. An outstanding book that will give Protestant readers a more thorough understanding of the Church.
Paperback, 192 pages (ISBN: 978-1-888212-28-0) CP Order No. 005216—$14.95*

Bread & Water, Wine & Oil
An Orthodox Christian Experience of God

by Fr. Meletios Webber

Worry, despair, insecurity, fear of death . . . these are our daily companions, and even though we attempt to ignore them or try to crowd them out, they are there, waiting for us in our quieter moments. It is precisely where we hurt most that the experience of the Orthodox Church has much to offer. The remedy is not any simple admonitions to fight the good fight, cheer up, or think positively. Rather, the Orthodox method is to change the way we look at the human person (starting with ourselves). Orthodoxy shows us how to "be transformed by the renewing of our mind"—a process that is aided by participation in the traditional ascetic practices and Mysteries of the Church. In this unique and accessible book, Archimandrite Meletios Webber first explores the role of mystery in the Christian life, then walks the reader through the seven major Mysteries (or sacraments) of the Orthodox Church, showing the way to a richer, fuller life in Christ.

Paperback, 200 pages (ISBN: 978-1-888212-91-4) CP Order No. 006324—$15.95*

A Beginner's Guide to Spirituality
The Orthodox Path to a Deeper Relationship with God

by Father Michael Keiser

Spirituality is in! Monks go platinum with recordings of chant, and books on self-help spirituality overflow supermarket bookracks. But what is the meaning of true spirituality? Aren't we all a little confused? Genuine spirituality keeps us in balance with God, our neighbor, and the material world. Fr. Michael Keiser walks us through the Orthodox Church's timeless teachings and practices on the ancient understanding of Christian spirituality with humor and keen insight. He outlines how ascetic practices, personal and corporate worship, confession and repentance, overcoming the passions, and opening ourselves up to God's grace can lead us to transformation, and to our ultimate destiny—Jerusalem, the heavenly city.

Paperback, 112 pages (ISBN: 978-1-888212-88-4) CP Order No. 007304—$10.95*

Let Us Attend!
A Journey Through the Orthodox Divine Liturgy

by Father Lawrence Farley

Esteemed author and Scripture commentator Fr. Lawrence Farley provides a guide to understanding the Divine Liturgy, and a vibrant reminder of the centrality of the Eucharist in living the Christian life.

Every Sunday morning we are literally taken on a journey into the Kingdom of God. Fr. Lawrence guides believers in a devotional and historical walk through the Orthodox Liturgy. Examining the Liturgy section by section, he provides both historical explanations of how the Liturgy evolved, and devotional insights aimed at helping us pray the Liturgy in the way the Fathers intended. In better understanding the depth of the Liturgy's meaning and purpose, we can pray it properly. If you would like a deeper understanding of your Sunday morning experience so that you can draw closer to God, then this book is for you.

Paperback, 104 pages (ISBN: 978-1-888212-87-7) CP Order No. 007295—$10.95*

*Plus applicable tax and postage & handling charges. Prices current as of 12/09. Please call Conciliar Press at 800-967-7377 for complete ordering information, or order online at www.conciliarpress.com.

Conciliar Media Ministries hopes you have enjoyed and benefited from this book. The proceeds from the sales of our books only partially cover the costs of operating our nonprofit ministry. We are committed to publishing high-quality books in a variety of formats with an Orthodox Christian worldview. Your financial support makes it possible to continue this ministry both in print and online. Donations are tax-deductible and can be made at www.conciliar-media.com.